YESTERDAY'S
WEST WIRRAL
~ Part One ~
Shotwick to Thurstaston
including:
Puddington Burton Ness Little Neston Neston
Parkgate Gayton Heswall Barnston Irby
~ A Pictorial History ~
1860 to 1960

Design & Origination: Ian Boumphrey

Published by: Ian Boumphrey The Nook 7 Acrefield Road Prenton
Wirral CH42 8LD Tel: 0151 608 7611

E-mail: ian@yesterdayswirral.co.uk

Website: www.yesterdayswirral.co.uk

Printed by: Graficas 94 HNOS Molina SL, Barcelona

ISBN: 978-1-899241-29-3

Price
£ 9.95

Bibliography

BC	The Buildings of England - Cheshire	N Pevesner & E Hubbard	1971
BIW	Burton in Wirral	Burton & South Wirral Local History Society	1984
BNVS	*Birkenhead News* Victory Souvenir of the Great War 1914-19		1919
BPV	Barnston Portrait of a Village	Colin Millington	2000
BW	*Birkenhead Wasp* - Theatrical and Athletic Gossip - vol 1-16		1892
DIR	Directory of Cheshire [other than Kelly's]		Various dates
DOS	History of the Diocese of Shrewsbury 1850-1986		1986
FYNC	Fifty Years of Neston Cricket	JH Gilling	1944
GUIDE	Guide book of the time		Various dates
HAFC	Heswall AFC 1891-1991		1991
HGC	Heswall Golf Club	Patrick Kenny	2001
HRC	Hoylake Racecourse and the Beginnings of the Royal Liverpool Golf Club		
		John Pinfold	2001
KD	Kelly's Directories		Various dates
LCP	Liverpool Courier Property Sales 1878-1907		1907
N	Neston 1840-1940	The Burton and S. Wirral History Society	1996
NEWS	Newspaper cuttings of the time		Various dates
NG	Ness Gardens	JK Hulme	1987
NS	Notes on Shotwick	FC Beazley	1915
NW	Neston at War 1939-1945	The Burton and Neston History Society	1999
OI	Old Irby	DM Young	1993
OP	Random Recollections of Old Parkgate	John Stonehouse	1889
OPB	Outline Plan for Birkenhead		1947
OTT	On The Turf	Phil Thompson	1991
PROG	Information taken from programmes of the time		Various dates
PWR	Portrait of Wirral Railways	Roger Jermy	1987
RLCHCH	Royal Liverpool County Hospital for Children at Heswall	Charles J Macalister	1930
RLGC	Royal Liverpool Golf Club	Guy B Farrah	1933
RSW	Railway Stations of Wirral	Merseyside Railway History Group	1994
SOTP	The School on the Puddydale 1909-1982	Jenny McRonald	1997
SOUV	Information taken from souvenir booklet		Various dates
T	Thurstaston	FC Beazley	1924
TCHWH	The Cheshire Hunts and Wirral Harriers	William Fawcett	1937
TDSC	The Dee Sailing Club	Commemorative Booklet 1982	1982
TDHT	The Diary of Henry Totty [Heswall farmer] 1868-1880		
		A Transcript by RS Cooper	2006
TGW	The Growth of Wirral	EH Rideout	1927
THW	The Hundred of Wirral	Philip Sulley	1889
THWKBL	The Hooton to West Kirby Branch Line	Merseyside Railway History Group	1982
TIL	The Ismay Line	Wilton J Oldham	1961
TP	This is Parkgate its buildings and story	The Parkgate & District Society	1979
TSP	The School on the Puddydale 1909-1982	Jenny McRonald	1997
TSSW	The Silver Screens of Wirral - A History of Cinemas in Hoylake, West Kirby and S Wirral		
		PA Carson and CR Garner	1990
Tv	Tingvelle	Greg Dawson	1993
TWCB	The Wirral Country Bus	TB Maund	2003
WBB	Wirral Bits and Bobs	Greg Dawson	2005
WDFA	Wirral District Football Association		1995
WHF	Wirral on the Home Front	Ian Boumphrey	2004
WM	*Wirral Magazine*	Various dates	1930s
WTDW	Where to Drink in Wirral	Birkenhead Brewery	1961
YW	Yesterday's Wirral [No. 1]	Ian & Marilyn Boumphrey	1980
YW6	Yesterday's Wirral No. 6	Ian & Marilyn Boumphrey	1991
YWPH	Yesterday's Wirral Pictorial History	Ian & Marilyn Boumphrey	2000

Introduction

This will be the sixth in my popular Yesterday's Wirral - Pictorial History series. This edition covers the area between Shotwick and Thurstaston including all the villages in between from Puddington to Burton, Ness, Little Neston, Parkgate, Leighton, Gayton, Heswall, Pensby, Irby, Thingwall, Barnston and the town of Neston. This is the fourth book covering this area - the other three being my first publication *Yesterday's Wirral - Neston, Parkgate and Heswall* plus *Yesterday's Wirral No.6 - Neston, Parkgate & Heswall + Thurstaston & Irby.* and *Yesterday's Wirral Pictorial History 1890 - 1953.* Although I used over 300 photographs in these three books, I have only used three of them in this publication - all the others here have not been published before by me and the majority have never been published by anyone.

I am particularly pleased to be covering this area in this my 29th year of publishing Wirral books, as I was born in Irby and spent the first 13 years of married life in Barnston.

It is hard to appreciate that in 1801 Neston was then the most important and largest populated place on Wirral with a population of 2,087 - Burton was the next largest with 288 - whereas the number of people in Birkenhead at the same time was 110. However, by 1861 Neston's population was 2,690 and Burton's had declined to 265, but Birkenhead's population had increased dramatically to 35,929.

The format in this publication is the same as the other books in this series which takes the reader through a century of life from the early / mid Victorian period through to the 1950s. I have used over 500 photographs and graphics, with captions for most images, also listing events and happenings - all in chronological order. The first image is a sketch, dating from c.1840, which shows the building that once stood on what is now the Donkey Stand at Parkgate. This building has been mentioned in most of the publications on Parkgate but to my knowledge a picture of it has never been published before.

The main occupations of the area up to the time of the First World War were servants, people working on farms and fishing - other types of work included mining at Little Neston. I have used many postcards and photographs which depicted thatched cottages and other old buildings including pubs, which were photographed before many of them were altered or demolished. Also many of the pictures show the way people used to dress, their method of transport and way of life. The later pictures indicate how the people and places changed as they moved further into the 20th century.

Most of the postcards and photographs in this book are from my collection, with a few of the pictures having no indication of the photographer and I apologise in advance for not acknowledging them. I have placed the images in or as near to the year as possible, but some postcards were posted several years after being published. When compiling a book of this kind, it is difficult to include every aspect of the area's history - however, I hope you approve of my selection.

Acknowledgements

**I would like to thank the following people who contributed towards the publication of this book
Sheila and Doug Baron, James Boumphrey, Marilyn Boumphrey, Larry Clow, Bill Collier,
Rob Cooper, Julie Dove, Ted Gerry, Gordale Nurseries, Anna Graham, Randall Grundy,
Gavin Hunter, Don and Chris Mackinnon, TB Maund, Betty Myers, Jill Nicholson, John Reeves,
Rosalie Williams**

1860

- The 11th Cheshire [**Neston**] Rifle Volunteers founded - three officers and 70 men[N]
- Infants school opened behind St Thomas' Church in **Parkgate**[N]

1861

- The Catholic School was built in **Neston** to accommodate 81 children[SOUV]
- A school was opened in the old vicarage High Street **Neston** which had ceased to be a vicarage in 1857[N]

1862

- *Ship Inn* **Parkgate** was rebuilt and enlarged - reopened as the *Union Hotel* [it reverted to its original name over 100 years later][TP]
- Jul 17 Birkenhead Joint Act passed for a branch railway from **Hooton** to **Parkgate**[PWR]

Population at 1861 Census - compared with 1801:

	1801	1861
Barnston	129	252
Birkenhead	110	35,929
Burton	288	265
Gayton	100	193
Heswall-cum-Oldfield	168	556
Irby	105	177
Leighton	266	363*
Ness	347	346**
Neston - Great	1,486	1,764*
Neston - Little	254	580
Pensby	22	38
Puddington	139	160
Shotwick	95	98
Shotwick Park	25	4
Thingwall	52	114
Thurstaston	112	123

*   Parkgate is included in Great Neston and Leighton
** Population at **Ness** had increased to 454 by 1851 but several houses had since been pulled down[TGW]

Above: *This sketch of **Parkgate** was taken from the original drawing by Charlotte Price c.1840*. It shows the building known as the Bath House, on the left beyond the pier, which once stood on the site of what is now known as the Donkey Stand. James Stonehouse's book* Random Recollections of Old Parkgate *1889 states that the water for the bath house was collected in large tanks on the beach when the tide was in and was pumped up to the bath house when required. Stonehouse's book also states "opposite the hotel* [The George] *was a long wooden pier [seen here] which ran far out into the river for the convenience of those engaged in boat sailing [see page 6]. There was another pier at the* Boathouse [the Pengwern Arms *in the distance] for the convenience of the passengers making use of the ferry to Flint and Bagillt. The remnants of these piers are still sticking up in the mud [1889]."*

*There seems to be some 'artist's licence' in this sketch as some of the buildings do not relate to the actual. The reason for this seems to be that Charlotte Price was a visitor to ***Parkgate*** and not local and also she would initially light pencil the drawing, then at a later date ink-in, without checking for accuracy

Above: *This 1850s sketch shows a row of* **Neston** *thatched houses with the* White Horse Inn *being the last one on the right [which can also be seen on page 9]. Originally built as houses, many of them were converted into shops and other businesses as demand grew from a growing population - some had single-storied extensions at the front as seen here. The first purpose-built shops were erected in the 1860s, eventually replacing all these old cottages - the* White Horse Inn *was re-built in 1877*

Above: Ashfield Hall, *was built in 1821 for John Winder Lyon Winder of* Vaynor Park *Montgomeryshire on his estate of about 240 acres. It was situated on the west side of Chester High Road* **Neston**, *near its present junction with Liverpool Road. The family were considerable land owners in Great and Little Neston, Leighton, Prenton and Willaston. This description was from Bagshot's Direstory of Cheshire 1850 "A beautiful house approached by a handsome portico with four handsome columns and delightfully situated in park-like grounds commanding good views of the River Dee and Welsh Hills" - it aptly described this print of the same period [see 1906]*

1863

– The Rev Richard Gleadowe built two semi-detached houses at **Parkgate** which later became *Holywell House Hotel*

1864

May 20 Thomas Johnson, the licensee of the *Pengwern Arms* **Parkgate** and the proprietor of the omnibus service from the hotel to Rock Ferry and Hooton, was drowned on the last recorded trip of the ferry service between the hotel and North Wales[N]

1865

– New police station and magistrate's room built in Park Street **Neston** next to the site of the present Methodist Church[N]

– A public well was sunk at the Cross in **Neston** - paid for by Christopher Bushell [see 1871][N]

– James Hegan erected a house at **Thurstaston** with some model farm buildings. Upon his death the estate was purchased by Thomas Ismay in 1877 [see text *Dawpool* 1884][TIL]

Apr 26 The centenary of the birth of Emma Hamilton at **Ness** - she later became Lady Hamilton [see photo] [NEWS]

Dec 30 Dawpool School was founded by deed in **Thurstaton**[SOUV]

Above: *Emily Lyon was born at **Ness** on 26 April 1765 and baptised at **Neston** 12 May 1765. She was the daughter of the blacksmith, but he died soon after her birth and was brought up by her grandmother in Hawarden. In her teens she went to work in **London** and being very beautiful had no problem getting suitors. After several relationships she married Sir William Hamilton and became Lady Emma Hamilton. She was most famous for becoming Lord Nelson's lover which they tried to hide - but everyone knew. She died in poverty, 10 years after Nelson, aged 50*

Above: *This sketch of the horse-drawn omnibus on The Parade at **Parkgate** in the 1860s was used as the letter heading for the* Pengwern Arms [The Boathouse, *situated at the north end of The Parade*], *which is in the author's possession [it was engraved and printed by Evans and Gresty of Eastgate Street Row Chester]. An 1860 directory states that "Thomas Johnston's omnibus leaves the* Boathouse [Pengwern Arms] *twice a day during the summer season for **Hooton** Station and for **Rock Ferry** every Tuesday and Saturday, calling in at the* Golden Lion Inn **Great Neston**". *Thomas Johnston, besides being the omnibus proprietor, was the licensee of* The Boathouse *and also listed as being a farmer - quite a busy man. The bath house pictured in the sketch on page four had been demolished with part of the site now the Donkey Stand to the right of the omnibus where two donkeys are waiting for customers. Also pictured there are two anchors. Beyond the Donkey Stand is the wooden pier for sailing boats [see the sketch on page four for details] opposite the* George Hotel. *The old* Assembly Room *is the tall white building pictured behind the omnibus which later had a balcony added and became known as* Balcony House

6

1866

–	The coach and horses service from **Hooton** to the *Pengwern Hotel* **Parkgate** ceased due to the new railway line opening from Hooton to Parkgate[N]
Sep	Cholera epidemic in the **Neston** area caused about 50 deaths this month[N]
Oct 1	Hooton to **Parkgate** railway single-line opened - about six miles long - with stations in **Little Neston** station and **Parkgate**[PWR]

1867

–	Christopher Bushell chaired the first Neston Local Board
Dec	Fire totally destroyed *Puddington Hall*[N]

1868

–	The Wirral Harriers were formed by John R Court who carried on the pack until passing it on in 1872[TCHWH]
Dec 19	The Wirral Harriers were reported passing through **Heswall** for the first time[TDHT]

Cheshire Omnibuses

These coach times were taken from *The Liverpool Guide* by James Stonehouse

To	Parkgate from Woodside Birkenhead daily on the arrival of the 4.30pm boat from Liverpool Fare inside 1/6d - outside 1/3d
From	Parkgate - Hooton 8am and 4.30pm sunday 6pm
From	Parkgate - Birkenhead daily at 8am

A directory of the time made the following observations:

Parkgate: *"Partly in the township of **Great Neston** and partly in that of **Leighton**, a place of considerable resort for sea bathing although from the receding of the tides from this shore it has lost much of its former importance. About fifty years ago Parkgate presented all the appearance of a seaport, there being at that time six packets besides other vessels constantly employed in the trade with Ireland. At the present period however, this as a packet station is completely neglected, as vessels beyond eight tons burthen cannot come within a considerable distance of the quay. A large sand-bank occupies the former channel. There is a communication with the Welsh coast by ferry boats. Here is a Coastguard Station consisting of Chief Boatman and three men."*

Great Neston: *"Is noted for the salubrity of air, which accounts for the longevity of many of its inhabitants. In the church-yard is a stone to the memory of John Hancock who attained the advanced age of 112, and his wife the age of 108 years. . . . .National Schools have recently been erected, and form a neat stone building for the accommodation of boys, girls and infants. They are situated on Liverpool Road, and were built at a cost of £2,000. The average attandance is 80 boys, 60 girls and 100 infants, The schools are so arranged as to form one large room, which is found most convenient for public meetings and lectures."*

Above: ***Thingwall*** *Mill was described in 1889 as being "one of the most conspicuous landmarks in Wirral and has been in the possession of the family of the Cappers for over 250 years. The ancient mill [pictured] was taken down and re-built in 1866. The inn adjoining [on the right], which also belongs to the same family, was also a very old structure" [see 1890 and 1898]*[THW]

1869

– First meeting of the Primitive Methodists in **Irby** held at *Irby Hill Farm* - the home of Mr and Mrs Cooke who had arrived at Irby two years previously [see 1887][YW6]

Apr 8 The **Chester, Neston** and Woodside Ferry District of Turnpike Roads and **Hinderton** and Birkenhead Turnpike Roads amalgamated at a meeting in the *Woodside Hotel* **Birkenhead**. The new title they took was United Trusts of Chester, Neston, Woodside and Hinderton and Birkenhead

Sep Mrs M Totty's house *Delavor House* built at **Heswall** [TDHT]

1870

– Robert Bridson started a threshing machine business in **Neston**. The business, which passed to his son George *c.*1898 and to George's son Thomas in 1932, expanded into steam ploughing engines, steam road locomotive traction engines and other engineering work - the business closed in 1967[N]

– Elementary school opened in **Little Neston** - replacing the church infants school

– **Burton** Parish Church restored[GUIDE]

– The school connected to Christ Church **Barnston** was opened - children were taught here for 80 years[SOUV]

Mar Work started on building **Heswall** Castle which was built for a Mr Titherington and was known locally as Tytherington's Folly. Erected on land at the corner of The Mount and Telegraph Road, it was said that his wife did not like the castle and they never moved in [see 1906][YW1]

Nov 29 The Parish of **Barnston** was formed out of the Parish of **Woodchurch**[SOUV]

Extracts from a Directory of the Time:

Heswall-cum-Oldfield: *Comprises the townships of Heswall and Gayton is a small village and township situated on an acclivity, on the Lower Division of the Wirral Hundred, 3 3/4 miles NNW from* **Great Neston**. *William Lloyd Esq and Arthur Henry Davenport Esq are the principal landowners and joint Lords of the Manor. Mr William Totty and Mr Thomas Hough are also proprietors, with numerous other small freeholders.*

Gayton: *Gayton in early times was possessed by the Gleggs, the heiress of whom, about the time of Henry VI, brought it in marriage to the Baskervilles, and they subsequently assumed the name Glegg. John Baskerville Glegg Esq is the owner of the whole township and Lord of the Manor [he resided at* Gayton Hall*]*

Above: *This old peg mill at* **Burton** *dated back to the 18th century but the first mill can be traced back to at least 1360. The mill was operated by turning the top wooden part on its stone base to face the prevailing wind by using a wooden shaft, which can be seen on a wheel [see 1886]*[N]

1871

– A fire at the *Royal Oak* **Little Neston** was put out - this was the first time they had used water from the Local Board Works[N]

– St Michael's Church **Shotwick** restored - the walls were raised by two courses of stone and a double span arch braced roof replaced the old single span roof[SOUV]

Mar 24 Several earthquake shocks felt at **Heswall**[TDHT]

Jun 30 Christ Church **Barnston**, which cost £3,000 to build, was consecrated[SOUV]

Aug 16 The whole Township of **Pensby** sold by JB Glegg to Mills and Fletcher of **Birkenhead** for £18,000 - it was then resold in small lots[TDHT]

Oct 29 Work began to build new school at **Heswall**[TDHT]

1872

– The Church School, School Hill **Lower Heswall** was opened[SOUV]

– *Black Horse Hotel* built in Village Road **Lower Heswall** - later changed its name to the *Heswall Hotel* and changed its name back to the *Black Horse Hotel* in 1940[YW6]

Oct 6 **Little Neston** Primitive Methodist Chapel opened - now **Little Neston** Methodist Church[SOUV]

Population at 1871 Census - compared with 1861:

	1861	1871
Barnston	252	292
Birkenhead	35,929	42,997
Burton	265	272
Gayton	193	188
Heswall-cum-Oldfield	556	722**
Irby	177	151
Leighton	363	334*
Ness	346	344
Neston - Great	1,764	1,856*
Neston - Little	580	662
Pensby	38	30
Puddington	160	165
Shotwick	98	92
Shotwick Park	4	11
Thingwall	114	125
Thurstaston	123	121

* Parkgate is included in Great Neston and Leighton
** Heswall increase given due to erection of villas by Liverpool merchants and others[TGW]

Above: *The thatched* White Horse Inn *is pictured at* **Neston** *Cross between 1865, when the wheel well was sunk at the expense of Christopher Bushell, and 1877 when this old thatched building was replaced [see page 12]. The far building on the right, with sign board above the top windows, was the* Golden Lion Hotel *in High Street whose licensee at this time was William Hancock. This was one of the more important hotels in Neston, as it was where passengers could take the omnibus which travelled between* **Parkgate** *and* **Rock Ferry Pier** *or* **Hooton** *Station. The hotel lost its licence in 1905*

1873

–   New school built at **Barnston** [the present Church Hall][BPV]

1874

–   During excavations for the rebuilding of **Neston** Parish Church, remnants of several Saxon Crosses were found[SOUV]

Apr   Charles Mott of **Birkenhead** leased land under the River Dee at **Ness** off the Earl of Shrewsbury and new shafts were sunk. A branch siding to convey the coal was provided by the London & North West and Great Western Railways and in 1875 planning permission was given to build houses for the colliers[N]

1875

–   Dee Lodge formed - they met at the *Union Hotel* **Parkgate**[N]

–   **Neston** Parish Church of St Mary and St Helen opened having been rebuilt at a cost of £8,000[N]

1875 continued

Sep 19   Lightening struck the weather vane of St Peter's Church **Lower Heswall** and passing into the body of the church, killed the deputising organist and a farm servant. The terrific storm also caused considerable damage to the building[SOUV]

1876

–   **Neston's** first public lights installed in Station Road and Park Street - these oil lamps were not operated in spring and summer to save money - being stored away until autumn[N]

–   New bridge built at **Barnston** - cost £629

May   An accident at **Neston** Colliery - two men were killed - Issac Fisher and a labourer named Hughes

Sep 1 to 17th - 41 people in **Neston** and **Parkgate** were stricken following a wave of cholera in the area - 27 died[OP]

Above: *This sketch [with some artist's licence], which was taken from the* Pengwern Arms *at **Parkgate**, shows horses pulling carts off the sands of the River Dee with familiar buildings in the background. The white building on the left is easily recognisable as the* Moorings *- it was one of only two buildings on the Parade at Parkgate with its gable end on. The wooden pier can be seen beyond the slipway and according to records was situated opposite the* George Hotel *[see opposite - now part of Mostyn House School] and was for local sailing boats [see 1860]*

Above: *The first coal mining operation had begun in Neston Parish in 1757 and ending in 1857. The **Neston** Colliery Company's workings, painted here by artist Arthur Suker in 1875, can be seen overlooking the River Dee. Another mine was opened nearby when a new shaft was sunk in 1874 and the mine operated here until in closed in 1927*

1877

– A third artesian well was sunk by Mostyn House School - this one still supplies the school today[N]

– Thomas Ismay bought the 390 acre estate of the late James Hegan at **Thurstaston** which had magnificent views over the River Dee and to the Welsh hills beyond. He did not care for the house, it was the position he loved [see 1882][TIL]

– Fresh borings at **Ness** Colliery in 1873 resulted in an entirely new winding house being erected with a new engine and more modern pumping apparatus installed. The building that was installed and even the Cornish beam engine that worked the pumps were still part of the operational equipment some 50 years later when mining ceased [see image previous page][NEWS]

– A school was established at **Puddington** - it had ceased by 1889[THW]

1878

– Following the erection of new equipment at **Ness** mine in 1877 and more miners employed there, it was decided to improve the 'shocking state' of the miners' cottages in the district. Many of the older hovels were demolished and two rows of cottages in New Street off Colliery Lane [later Marshlands Road] were erected about this time by the Neston Colliery Company. There were a total of 38 terraced cottages in two blocks with each cottage having two rooms downstairs and two bedrooms upstairs and a long shed at the back which served as a communal toilet - it was said that youngsters would go round the back of the toilets and tickle people from behind with a feather on a stick! [see 1957]

1879

– St Peter's Church Lower Village **Heswall** rebuilt [see 1875][SOUV]

Above: *The* George Inn, *which is pictured in The Parade* **Parkgate** *dated back to at least 1779 when it was first recorded with Joseph Manlove being the landlord. He also offered his new bathing machine with a 'modesty hood' to ladies advertising it thus: "Ladies may bathe with the utmost ease and secrecy. Every lady will, if desired, be attended with a female servant". Thomas Spencer, Joseph Manlove's son-in-law, became the next licensee until 1808 when Daniel Briscoe took over. Upon his death, his widow Esther enlarged and refurbished the inn, re-opening it as the* Mostyn Arms Inn *in 1819[DIR]. She successfully ran the hotel for over 35 years until her death in 1855 when it was purchased by Edward Price who owned a school in Tarvin and transferred it here, calling it Mostyn House School. The Rev AS Grenfell, nephew of Edward Price, took over the school in 1862. It must have been in a poor state as Mrs Grenfell declared "I had never seen such a horrible hole in all my life". The numbers of boys, who were aged between 10 and 15, varied between 30 and 60. AS Grenfell's eldest son Algernon became headmaster in 1890 and saved the school by improving the state of the buildings and changing it into a preparatory school [see 1906]*

1880

- Joseph Mealor set up business as a plough maker in **Ness**[N]
- The Dawpool Estate **Thurstaston** was purchased by Thomas H Ismay, founder of White Star Line, who demolished the house and replaced it with the mansion *Dawpool* [see text 1884][THW]

Apr 8 **Neston's** first election day for 40 years was held between Conservatives and Liberals. As anticipated fighting broke out early afternoon and by dusk police reinforcements had arrived from **Birkenhead** but they were outnumbered by the stone-throwing rabble of over 1,000. It was not until a local Magistrate read the Riot Act that fighting stopped and the crown dispersed[NEWS]

Jun 16 *Hill Cottage* Rocky Lane **Heswall** sold at auction £350, *Hill Lodge*, Rocky Lane **Heswall** sold £350 and *Hill House* Telegraph Road sold £1,500 [LCPSR]

Jul 3 **Barnston** Vicarage completed and first used[SOUV]

Above: *The* Sawyer's Arms *The Parade* **Parkgate** *is the building with the inn sign above the door. The first licensee was probably Richard Bartley, a carpenter and Sawyer [hence the name], who held an aleseller's licence in 1793. However, in 1905 it lost its licence and the inn closed. The buildings on the left were part of the* Dee Cottages *and* Pengwern *was the house on the right*

Left: *This was the new* White Horse Inn *pictured at* **Neston** *Cross with the High Street to the right. It replaced the original inn in 1877, using part of the old building [see page 9]. The inn closed in the 1960s*

Right: *This early photograph of* The Watch House *on* The Parade *at* **Parkgate** *was taken before the building was rendered. It shows the different type of material used in its construction with the latest bricks top right being different to the others - could this have been an extension to the first floor of the house? Whether this was the family who lived in the* Watch House *or just posing for the photographer, they seem well dressed - perhaps it was for Sunday or a special occasion [see 1954]*

- Dr Riddock founded the Literary and Debating Society in **Parkgate**[N]
- **Neston** and **Parkgate** Gas Company formed[N]
- Wm Flemming established his building business in **Neston**[N]
- Census showed that 147 men were working at **Ness** Colliery[N]
- The Wirral Hunt Club held its first annual steeplechase meeting at Parks Field **Parkgate** [see sketch][HRC]
- A great storm damaged many fishing boats at **Parkgate** - they were repaired by the landlord of *Red Lion* Parkgate who had been a ship's carpenter[N]
- The Primitive Methodist Tin Chapel opened in the stackyard opposite **Irby** Hill [Dodd's] Farm - cost £130 [see 1930][OI]
- Thomas Ismay, founder of the White Star Line, had his portrait painted by John [later Sir John] Millais - at the expense of the shareholders of White Star Line - he lived at *Dawpool* **Thurstaston** [see 1911][TIL]

Feb 11 *Nag's Head* ph. + over 1 acre land **Neston** sold at auction £850 - also *The Malt Shovel* bh. and cottage Liverpool Road **Neston** £330 - also *Coach and Horses* ph. **Neston** sold £610[LCPSR]

Sep 23 *The Malt Shovel* bh. and cottage Liverpool Road **Neston** sold at auction £345 [making £15 profit, having bought it in February][LCPSR]

Above: *The Wirral Hunt Club held an annual steeplechase meeting at **Parkgate** from 1881 until 1897 when it was transferred to **Hooton** Park. This sketch by Harry B Nielson shows racegoers travelling to the Parkgate races by all modes of transport. In his book* Auld Lang-Syne *he recalled "the race meeting at Parkgate was like a jolly old-fashioned picnic. There were no enclosures, and people from **Birkenhead**, **Claughton** and **Oxton** and round about made up family parties and big tuck hampers, and drove to the course in all sorts of conveyances, 'buses, wagonettes, open hired cabs, etc. Two or three slap-up coaches and four-in-hand drags gave an old-time touch to the scene." Although the race meetings were held on the old Parkgate course on Parks Field up to the Wood Lane boundary, they were officially called the **Great Neston** Races*

Population at 1881 Census - compared with 1871:

	1871	1881
Barnston	292	280
Birkenhead	42,997	51,610
Burton	272	257
Gayton	188	199
Heswall-cum-Oldfield	722*	876
Irby	151	154
Leighton	334	259*
Ness	344	376
Neston - Great	1,856	2,119*
Neston - Little	662	1,018
Pensby	30	30
Puddington	165	158
Shotwick	92	77
Shotwick Park	11	14
Thingwall	125	162
Thurstaston	121	113

*Parkgate is included in Great Neston and Leighton[TGW]

Above: *The* Plough Inn *is pictured in Park Street **Neston** at its junction with Cross Street when William Hughes was the licensee. The inn closed during the First World War [see page 57]*

– Deeside Electric Works opened in **Neston** on an ancient roadway from Moorside to the old quay by GC Taylor and Company [see etching]. The company later moved to a site in **Helsby** eventually becoming British Insulated Callender Cables [BICC][N]

– **Neston** gas works opened in Church Lane - street lights lit by gas for the first time - replacing oil[N]

– Joseph Johnson opened his plumbing and painting business in Parkgate Road **Neston** - in 1892 he opened an ironmongers shop in High Street Neston[N]

– **Burton** windmill partially destroyed during a gale - this old peg mill dated back to 1629 [see page 8][BIW]

– Bushell Fountain erected at The Cross **Neston** on the site of a well sunk at the expense of and named after Christopher Bushell, a local benefactor [see 1894][N]

Jul 7 *The Lidgetts* and land 'Barncroft' - over 1 acre **Lower Heswall** sold at auction - the house £810 and land £490[LCPSR]

Jul 12 Act for **Parkgate** to **West Kirby** railway extension passed[APWR]

Jul 26 The Mayor of **Birkenhead** [William Laird] and Corporation of Birkenhead took possession of that portion of **Thurstaston** Hill which had been claimed for public recreation and walked the boundaries[HWKD]

Jul 29 Thomas Ismay and his wife Margaret laid the foundation stone for their new house *Dawpool* at **Thurstaston** - having demolished the existing one[TIL]

Sep 30 Convalescent home opened by the Duke of Westminster initially for 13 patients [men and boys only] on The Parade **Parkgate** for the **Chester** Royal Infirmary - it was estimated that when the new wing was completed it would accommodate a further 14 patients[OP]

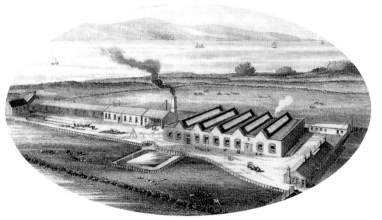

Right: *This is a sketch of the Dee Side Electric Works **Neston**, situated in what was later known as Quay Lane. They were established here, overlooking the River Dee with the Welsh hills in the background, in 1882 by GC Taylor & Co. The main business was insulating cables and due to their success they moved to Helsby in 1887 and later renamed the company British Insulated Callenders Cables [BICC]. The reasons they gave for moving from here was the poor railway system and lack of suitable local employees [see 1909]*[N]

Above: *The children of **Heswall** School are posing for the photographer at the Church of England School on School Hill. They moved here from the previous school in The Village, opposite the* Black Horse Hotel *in Lower Heswall 10 years previously in 1872. The girl third from from right on the back row, with a flower on her blouse was Emily Boumphrey, a relative of the author [see Sergeant Bee of **Neston** 1920]*

1883

– Reports in the local newspapers stated that over 60 policemen were needed to control an over zealous crowd at the **Great Neston** races. There was much drunkenness, pick-pocketing and other petty crimes - this resulted in the local magistrates refusing an alcoholic licence for the 1888 meeting[OTT]

Aug 26 Foundation stone laid for **Parkgate** and **Neston** Presbyterian Church in Parkgate Road on the corner of Moorside Lane on land donated by Mr J Johnson Houghton of **Thornton Hough**[SOUV]

1884

– New bells provided for **Neston** Parish Church[N]
– The round **Hinderton** water tower was built on land donated by Christopher Bushell - using stone from his quarry[N]
– A miner's strike at **Neston** Colliery resulted in the Neston Colliery Company at **Ness** going into liquidation[N]

Jul 18 **Parkgate** and **Neston** Presbyterian Church in Parkgate Road on the corner of Moorside Lane erected at a cost of £3,000 - the walls were of Storeton stone and Yorkshire shoddies[SOUV]

Aug 25 Three men were drowned when the boat they had sailed in from **Parkgate** to Flint, had capsized having run aground on a sand bank on the return journey - two others were saved[OP]

Oct 16 Mr Gladstone performed the 'cutting of the sod of the Wirral Railway'

Dec *Dawpool*, the new residence of the Ismay family - owners of White Star Line, was completed at **Thurstaston** - this was to commemorate their 25th wedding anniversary[TIL]

Left: *The two horses are standing outside the* Royal Oak *at* **Little Neston** *which faced the Village Green to the right. This inn dated back to at least 1822 when the licensee was Samuel Hancock but by 1828 it was Sarah Hancock - wife or daughter of Samuel [see 1892]*

Above: Irby *Hall pictured here in Irby Road was built in the 17th century. It was restored in 1888 when the bottom half of the half-timbered hall was replaced with stone. The original building was the ancient manor house of Saint Werburgh's Abbey* **Chester** *and was the home of the Glegg family*

1885

- Bushell Road **Neston** completed - linked Neston Station with Hinderton Road - Christopher Bushell, a local landowner, gave £400 towards the cost[N]
- St Bartholomew's Church **Thurstaston** rebuilt[BC]
- Windmill - Leighton Road **Neston** ceased grinding corn [see 1934][N]
- **Gayton** Mill ceased working[SOUV]
- The *Pengwern Arms* **Parkgate** demolished [see 1938][YW6]

Apr 16 L & NW and GWR opened the railway extension from **Parkgate** to **West Kirby**

1886

- The Wirral Colliery Company was the new company set up to run **Neston** Colliery[N]

Jan 5 Thomas Ismay, Chairman of White Star Line, entertained the Prince of Siam at his home *Dawpool* at **Thurstaston** - later that year he entertained Queen Victoria aboard the ferry *Claughton* when she came to open the Exhibition in **Liverpool**[TIL]

Jan 7 St Bartholomew's Church **Thurstaston** was consecrated[SOUV]

Apr 19 **Parkgate** to **West Kirby** railway extension opened - the line was then 19 miles long from **Hooton to West Kirby**– with new railway stations opened at **Parkgate, Heswall** and **Thurstaston** - Parkgate old station closed and became the goods yard [see text this page][APWR]

The building of the Parkgate to West Kirby railway extension 1884-86

Work began on building the extension in 1884. The Chester Chronicle *describes the navvies who built the line:* "The withdrawal of such a heavy contingent of navvies, say from 300 to 400, from the vicinity of **Neston,** will have a serious effect on the local trade. It should be stated, in justice to these men, that they have conducted themselves with great decorum during their stay in the vicinity and it is worthy of note how rarely have the navvy men had to appear before the Magistrates at their monthly sessions. It must be a great satisfaction to those who have taken an interest in these men to find how good has been their conduct. Whenever a delinquent has been obliged to appear in court who has been designated himself a 'navvy', nine times out of ten the culprit has turned out to be a **Liverpool, Birkenhead** or **Chester** loafer or corner man so hard up that as to be obliged to work for a few days to put him in funds for a much coveted debauch. The real navvy born and bred is a different breed of man".*

The opening of the extension of the railway from Hooton to West Kirby

The Chester Chronicle *describes the opening of the extension:* "On Good Friday **Parkgate** was thronged with people. It is said that so many have not been seen for years assembling on the Esplanade. The opening of the Parkgate Extension Line brought shoals of holiday folks to avail themselves of the accommodation. **West Kirby** was also very full of guests. The delightful weather drew everybody out of doors".*

Above: *A Victorian tea party is taking place by the side of the ruins of the old peg mill at **Burton** which dated back to the 18th century [see 1869]. It ceased operating having been partially destroyed following a strong gale c.1877. Most of the wooden remains, including the wheels which are seen on top of the framework, had been taken down by the turn of the century [see 1902]*[N]

1887

–   'Ismay Cutting' was a re-routed road cut into the sandstone at **Thurstaston** at the expense of Thomas Ismay, the Chairman of White Star Line, who did not want traffic in front of his newly built mansion *Dawpool* [see 1910]

Feb 8   Two houses opposite the Rectory **Lower Heswall** + land sold at auction £800[LCPSR]

Apr   The *Boathouse* [*Pengwern Arms*] **Parkgate** was badly damaged during a storm amd later demolished[RROP]

1888

–   **Irby** Hall was reconstructed - originally it was all half-timbered [see page 15]

Jan 23 Bruce Ismay and his recent American bride, Florence, arrived at the family home *Dawpool* **Thurstaston** - they celebrated with a large bonfire on the cricket ground, a firework display and dancing on the green to music from the Hoylake Band[TIL]

Mar 15 *Windle Hill* **Neston** 5 acres sold at auction £760[LCPSR]

Above: *This was a rear view of **Irby** Hill Farm with the entrance to the farm yard between the two men and the rear of the farmhouse behind the man sitting down. The farm was run by Mr and Mrs Cooke who came here from Knutsford. It was in the farmhouse in 1869 that they held the first meeting of the Primitive Methodists in Irby. By 1881 the congregation had outgrown the farmhouse and the tin chapel was erected across the road in the Stack Yard [see 1930]*

Above: *The* Greyhound Inn *pictured on the left in **Shotwick** village had the sign of a black greyhound above the door. There was an inn mentioned in Shotwick in 1561 and again in 1673. The inn was still operating in 1896 when Peter Wilkinson was the licensee. History would probably have passed by this small rural inn had it not been for three Irish labourers travelling from **Chester** towards **Parkgate** for the boat back to Ireland on 29 August 1750. Two of them attacked the third near **Saughall** Mill, killed him and stole his money. Instead of making their way directly to Parkgate, they stopped off for a drink at the* Greyhound Inn *at Shotwick, where they tried to rob the licensee. However, she caught them and called the authorities, who by this time had found the dead body of their companion and were looking for the other two. One of the two gave evidence against the other one. They were both found guilty at Chester Assizes and hanged at Boughton near Chester on 22 September 1750. It was said that the two bodies were then hung up in irons near Two Mills [named after two medieval water mills in **Puddington** and Shotwick] on the heath and a gibbet made on an ash tree at the junction of Parkgate Road and a path near the Saughall Mill. They were left here to deter their fellow countrymen who had committed many offences in that part of the county. To this day Saughall Mill is sometimes referred to as the 'Gibbet Mill'*

1889

– *Leighton Court* Buggen Lane **Neston** built for a Liverpool stockbroker George O'Neill-Bridge but he only lived there for two years. It was later purchased by Mr Whineray who used outbuildings to manufacture munitions during the First World War [see 1916][YW6]

Feb **Neston** Town Hall opened[N]

May 20 **Parkgate** Convalescent Home had admitted 1,495 patients since it opened 30 September 1882[OP]

1890

– AG Grenfell became headmaster of Mostyn House School **Parkgate** - there were only 30 pupils and a decaying building - within five years numbers were up to 100

– A garden party at *Dawpool* **Thurstaston** was given by the Ismay family and later the annual sports day on the Dawpool Cricket ground was attended by 2,000 people[TIL]

Jun 6 *Hill Cottage* Rocky Lane **Heswall** sold at auction £290 - also *Hill House* Telegraph Road sold £2,050 [see text 1880][LCPSR]

Above: *The* **Thingwall** *Mill pictured here with a reefing stage was the replacement for the ancient mill [see 1866] which was taken down and rebuilt in 1866. The building on the right, described in 1889[THW] as a very old structure, was the* Mill Inn *which was owned by the Capper family who were also the millers. Besides these two buildings there was nothing else of interest in the township and no evidence of this being the suposed centre of the Viking settlement [see 1898]*

Left: *The children playing a game are probably from* **Parkgate** *Infants School which was behind St Thomas's Church in the Square. They are seen in front of the* Union Hotel *[later renamed the* Ship Inn] *on the left and the door on the right belonged to Mostyn House School*

Above: *Looking down Chester High Road towards* **Chester** *when it was a narrow road. The* Glegg Arms *at* **Gayton**, *which took its name from the Glegg family who owned Gayton Estate from 1330 to 1921, is pictured on the left. The inn was built c.1840 and was once named 'Crabb's Inn' after Edward Crabb who was listed in 1850 as wheelwright and victualer. The publican of the inn at the time of this photograph was J Brownlie[DIR]*

1891

- The Church of the Good Shepherd was built in Telegraph Road **Heswall**
- Wesleyan Chapel opened in Telegraph Road **Heswall** - cost £1,450 - later became known as the Methodist Church [see 1907]
- **Heswall** AFC founded - based at the *Black Horse Hotel* and their pitch was down 'Dick' Manners Lane by the railway line. They initially played friendlies but then joined the Wirral District Association [see 1902][HAFC]
- A tablet fixed to the wall of *Wellfield House* Wall Rake **Lower Heswall** stated: "Site of the Hessle Well. Closed by permission of the Wirral Highway Board 1891"[WM]

Jan 22 *White Lion Inn* **Lower Heswall** + over 7 acres land **Neston** sold at auction £4,750 [see 1902][LCP]

*Above: The chalk board held by the boy at the front says; 'Dawpool School 1891 - Group III'. The school was built in what is now Station Road in 1858 by Joseph Hegan, the then owner of the Dawpool Estate. In 1860 there were 70 children being taught by here by Mr MA Jeffrey. In 1902, the school became known as Dawpool National School. The school moved to new premises in School Lane **Thurstaston** in January 1906, which was funded by Mrs Margaret Ismay in memory of her Husband Thomas Ismay [see 1906]*

Population at 1891 Census - compared with 1881:

	1881	1891
Barnston	280	404
Birkenhead	51,610	58,287
Burton	257	266
Gayton	199	199
Heswall-cum-Oldfield	876	1,210
Irby	154	174
Leighton	259	325*
Ness	376	354
Neston - Great	2,119	2,240*
Neston - Little	1,018	1,012
Pensby	30	51
Puddington	158	150
Shotwick	77	77
Shotwick Park	14	8
Thingwall	162	173
Thurstaston	113	145

*Parkgate is included in Great Neston and Leighton[TGW]

*Above: The cottage on the left [now two storeys] stood at the top of Station Road **Burton** with Burton Road bending to the right and leading to **Ness** and **Neston***

*Left: The Brewer's Arms **Neston** dates back to at least 1732 when it was named on the Mostyn Estate Map. In 1828 the licensee was William Hughes [there were 12 licenced premises listed in Neston at that time][DIR]*

1892

– The Wirral District Association Football League formed with two divisions and a Junior League - known as the Wirral League [today it is the West Cheshire League][HAFC]

May 26 *Ship Inn* and shop **Lower Heswall** sold at auction £1,400[LCP]

Sep The adjoining *Black Bull* and *Greenland Fisheries* **Neston** were acquired and merged by a Chester brewery – and became the *Greenland Fisheries*[BW]

Dec 25 Skating took place at **Parkgate** on Christmas Day following a spell of Arctic weather [see 1895]

Below: *The* Royal Oak, *pictured facing the Village Green at* **Little Neston***, dated back to at least 1822 when the victualler was listed as Samuel Hancock[DIR] but by 1828 it had been passed to Sarah Hancock - probably Samuel's wife or daughter [see 1883]. The inn suffered fire damage in 1871 and again in 1901, when it was rebuilt - the building still faces the Village Green [see 1903]*

1893

– Mostyn House Preparatory School for boys **Parkgate** formed a cadet corps which was attached to the 1st Batallion, Cheshire Regiment - the boys wore similar uniforms to the men and also had rifles [see 1904][NEWS]

– The **Neston** Telephone Exchange opened in Mrs Youd's Confectioner's shop - by 1899 there were 31 connections

– The house *Roscote* in Wall Rake was altered and enlarged for Thomas Brocklebank[BC]

Jun 28 Oldfield Common **Lower Heswall** [part] over 2 acres sold at auction £220 - also 3,165 sq. yds. at 9d [4p] per sq. yd. and 4,952 sq. yds at 9.5d per sq. yd. *Rowlands Hey* **Lower Heswall** - over 2 acres sold at auction £121 - also *Oldfield Farm* [part] over 18 acres sold at auction £1,400[LCP]

Oct 17 *The Wheat Sheaf* ph. **Ness** + 5 acres land sold at auction £2,100[LCP]

Oct 18 *Denhall* **Ness** 14 acres sold at auction[LCP]

Left: *Looking down Dee View Road* **Heswall** *the people are standing by the entrance to the* Dee View Inn. *In 1874 the beer retailer was Joseph Ellis who was also listed as a smallware dealer. It was taken over by Birkenhead Brewery [see 1928]. The building beyond was once a branch Mackie and Gladstone and the site now forms part of the car park [see 1914]*

1894

- **Neston** Cricket Club founded by Dr Henry Speechly [see 1895][N]
- Moorland House School was founded in **Heswall** by a Mr Dobie [see photo 1904]
- The Church of England School [mixed] School Hill **Heswall**, reported an average attandance of 230 - which was the capacity of the school at that time

Feb 11 The churchyard cross of St Winefried's Roman Catholic Church, Burton Road **Neston** was blown down in a severe storm - it was then replaced being erected by 'the young men and maidens of St Winefride's 1894'[SOUV]

Sep 30 **Neston**-Cum–**Parkgate** Urban District formed out of the former township of **Great Neston** and **Leighton** - part of **Little Neston** transfered to **Raby**[TGW]

*Above right: **Gayton** Windmill, which is seen from Telegraph Road, is in a neglected state with the boat-shaped wooden roof partly intact with the wheel still there. It was said to be Wirral's oldest tower mill dating back to the 16th century when it was owned by the Glegg family of Gayton Hall. In 1850 the corn millers were Samuel and James Woodward - it was last operated c.1860 [see 1902]*

*Left: Looking down **Neston** High Street from The Cross where the drinking fountain can be seen which was erected in 1882 at the expense of Christopher Bushell. The Parish Church of St Mary and St Helen is seen in the background with work to the right of the cross in High Street being carried out in connection with the public weighing machine*

*Right: Stivelooms is the near building in Village Road **Lower Heswall** at its junction with Station Road off to the left. The thatched cottage beyond was split into two with the near two thirds known as 'Stacey's Cottage' and was used as an office for Mr Roberts the registrar. This cottage was demolished between the wars and the site is now part of the garden for Stivelooms [see 1922][YW6]*

1895

- Neston Cricket Club played their first few matches at *Leighton Banastre* but then moved to their present ground at Parkgate
- Jackson's Tower in the centre of **Neston** built for George Jackson whose chemist shop was next door [see photo 1906][YW6]

Dec 11 Stone Quarry - over 2 acres Telegraph Road **Heswall** sold at auction £725 - plus 1 acre sold £500 - also shop, cottage and abattoir Lower Village **Heswall** £620 - also smithy and workshop Lower Village **Heswall** £255[LCPSR]

Above: *Neston Cricket Club was founded in 1894 and initially the club is said to have played its matches in the grounds of* Leighton Banastre. *Its founder and first captain Dr Speechly [the wicket keeper] is playing a match on the **Parkgate** ground with schoolboys probably from Mostyn House School. This main ground was purchased in 1922 and in 1977 the rear field was bought from Mostyn House School[FYNC]*

Above: *The* Fox and Hounds *at **Barnston** appears in records from at least 1850 when the victualler was listed as Joen Stubbs and in 1860 John Gerbrey. The inn was replaced in 1910 with the present building [see 1931]*

Above: *In February of 1895 the River Dee resembled a vast ice field which stayed for several weeks before thawing - seen here at **Parkgate***

- Neston and Parkgate Hygenic Laundry and Cleaning Co was formed, opening in **Neston**[N]
- Fire brigade established in **Neston** with eight men and a captain - using a manual engine purchased from **Liverpool**[N]
- **Puddington** Methodist Chapel built[OPB]
- Cheshire County Council erected mileposts on the Chester High Road - they replaced the sandstone milestones which were eventually rescued by AG Grenfell of Mostyn House School **Parkgate** and can be seen on the school drive
- The last Wirral Hunt Steeplechase was held on Parks Field **Parkgate**[N]

Jan 8   Cottage adjoining **Thingwall** windmill sold at auction £200 [see photo][LCPSR]

Jul 21 **Ness** Estate sold at auction - including:- *Friendship Farm* **Ness** over 13 acres sold £570 [see photo 1904] - *Haddon Hall Farm* 206 acres sold £6,025 and land in 16 lots for £5,000[LCPSR]

Aug   Plot of land in Telegraph Road **Heswall** opposite the Puddydale purchased by the Presbyterian Church of England and the 'Tin Tabernacle' erected on the site[YWPH]

Above: *Irby Mill in a ruinous state with the* Miller's Cottage *behind [see page 25]*

Above: *The* Mill Inn *cottage adjoining* **Thingwall** *windmill was sold at auction in 1897 for £200*

Above: ***Shotwick*** *Hall, seen from the main gate, was built by Joseph Hockenhull of* **Hockenhull** *and* **Shotwick** *in 1622. The window frames are of wood, mullioned and transomed and under relieving arches*[C]

Above: *Bishop Wilson's Cottage* **Burton** *dated back to at least 1663 when Thomas Wilson was born here - about the time the thatched cottage was rebuilt*

Left: *The* Glegg Arms, *which is pictured at* **Gayton** *at the start of the Chester High Road, was built c.1840 and takes its name from the Glegg family who owned Gayton Estate. The single-storied building jutting out on the left, with a post box in the wall, was the office for the weighbridge which can be seen on the road beneath the window [see page 18]*[DIR]

— The infants' school at **Parkgate** which could accommodate 70 children had an average attendance of 48[KD]

Apr 30 The *Union Hotel* **Parkgate** sold at auction £5,100[LCPSR]

Jul 6 *Dale House Farm* - with over 7 acres of land - **Barnston** sold at auction £1,200[LCPSR]

Jul 15 *New House Farm* **Puddington** 188 acres sold at auction £6,350 - also *Chapel House Farm* Puddington 135 acres £5,000 - also School House etc Puddington £255[LCPSR]

Jun 18 Thomas Ismay of *Dawpool* **Thurstaston** - founder of the White Star line declined the honour of a knighthood[TIL]

Below: *Joseph Boumphrey [a relative of the author] is seen working as a stonemason. He was one of the stonemasons who repaired St Peter's Church Tower **Heswall** following the great storm of 1875. His father, Joseph, also a stonemason repaired the same tower in the late 1840s and is recorded as having been paid £19 and Joseph Smallwood, a blacksmith, £6. The family can be dated back to Gayton in 1690 when another Joseph Boumphrey was also listed as a stonemason [see below]*

Below Left: *This is reputed to be the horse and cart belonging to Joseph Boumphrey outside the* Glegg Arms **Gayton** *who is probably one of the men in the picture [see other photo]*

Above: *These Victorian families are promenading on The Parade at **Parkgate**, with some of them walking along the slightly raised wall - just as families do today. The building on the left behind the cart is* The Moorings, *which is still there today and is one of only two houses on The Parade which has a gable end fronting the river[TP]*

Left: *Mrs Cooke, the farmer's wife of* Irby Hill Farm *[see 1887], is standing on the opposite side of Mill Hill Road* **Irby** *from the farm, whose outbuildings are seen on the right. The narrow road led towards* **Greasby** *[Irby Cricket Club is now on the right beyond the outbuildings]*

Below: Rookery Farm *is seen on the right in* **Irby** *village - the building in the distance was* Corner House Farm *at the junction of Thurstaston Road and Irby Road*

Below: *The little girl is standing in front of* **Irby** *Mill which had ceased operating in 1875. This had been the second mill in the immediate area, built between 1709 and 1725, with the first mill dating back to at least 1291 and erected on the other side of Hill Bark Road, behind the photographer, near the quarry. This post mill was operated by turning the top wooden structure, so that the sails faced the prevailing wind, by turning it on its brick base using the wooden lever on a wheel which is seen in front of the* Miller's Cottage *in the background [see page 23]*

- Arthur Killpin Bulley built his house *Mickwell Brow* at **Ness** - later to become Ness Gardens [see 1905][N]
- **Irby** Mill, a post mill erected on a brick base 1709-25 said to have been demolished [see previous page][YWPH]
- Due to the building of a new railway station at **Heswall Hills** - an application was applied for a new pub to be called *The Railway Inn* to be built on the corner of Brimstage Road and Acre Lane. Mainly due to the objection of the Glegg Estate [they owned the *Glegg Arms* at **Gayton**] the application was turned down. However, the house *The Coppice,* which was still built but with no licence, is still there today

May 1 **Heswall Hills** Railway Station opened[PWR]

Above: *Irby Hill Farm in Irby Hill Road **Irby** had their own water supply, as the girl is seen pumping water - others had to go to the nearest well which was in **Frankby**. These farm buildings were converted into houses more recently*

Above: *The derelict **Thingwall** Mill, pictured here, was rebuilt in 1866 as the replacement for the ancient mill which dated back to c.1640. The mill had started to fall into disrepair when it ceased operating in 1886 [see page 7]*

Above: *The two whitewashed cottages, pictured here with outbuildings, still stand today in Barnston Dale Barnston Road **Barnston**. When the road was widened the two outbuildings were demolished - the far one belonging to Ralph Robinson, a wheelwright who is said to have once built a cart and upon completion found it was too big to leave his yard! The local source of water until the First World War was the well in the Dale, which was accessed through the wall on the right - in the far distance[YW1]*

Right: *These ancient thatched cottages were pictured in Well Lane off Burton Road **Ness** - near the Wheatsheaf Inn. They were demolished and replaced by a row of terraced houses named Sunset Cottages[YW1]*

– The single-storied Post Office building in **Lower Heswall** opened [see 1903]

– There were 23 subscribers to the **Heswall** Telephone Exchange which was based in Bank Buildings - they had moved to new premises in The Mount by 1906

May **Dawpool** Cricket Club, in the grounds of *Dawpool* opened their new pavilion - Lady Margaret Ismay was the scorer[NEWS]

Aug 1 **Burton** Point Station opened[PWR]

Nov 23 Thomas Ismay, Chairman of the White Star Line died - he was buried at **Thurstaston** - he left £1,297,881 in his will - £25,000 to charities and the rest to his family[TH]

Dec15 Following his brave action at the battle of Colenso, South Africa, Walter Congreve of **Burton** Hall was awarded the VC [see text 1916][NEWS]

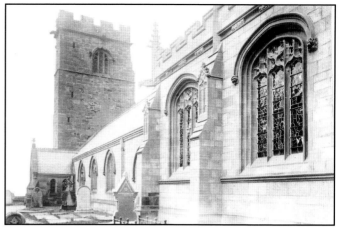

Above: *The tower of St Peter's Parish Church* **Lower Heswall** *shows the signs of repair following the storms of 1847 and 1875 [see 1916]. The first church on this site dated back to c.1300 and survived until 1737 when the then minister Rev John Morris set about replacing most of the old structure, with only the tower remaining from the old one. Following the great storm of 1875, the present church was built - again only the tower remained from the old church*

The *Heswall Hotel* Village Road Lower Heswall was tenanted by Mr Leeman from 1898 to 1910 and his son, Jack Leeman remembered it had 13 bedrooms, three private sitting rooms, an attractive public dining room and a billiards room. He remembered his mother made a speciality of ham and eggs teas for 1/6d on a Sunday which was popular with ramblers and cyclists - there were no buses and very few private cars - but there was a railway station at Heswall. In 1940 it reverted to its original name - the *Black Horse Hotel*

Above: *Irby* Village is seen when Thingwall Road was a dirt track with no pavements. The Prince of Wales Inn *is seen in the distance - built about 1880 it was only licenced as a beerhouse unlike the other inn in the village,* The Anchor, *which was fully licenced. The* Prince of Wales *lost its licence about 1920 when the Peers family ran it. During the Second World War the building was used as the headquarters of the Home Guard and was demolished in the 1950s. Today the site is a car park adjoining the Post Office. The nearest building is the only one still there today with the thatched building beyond being the Post Office [see 1902]*

1900

- First annual summer camp of artillerymen held at Parks Field **Parkgate** - last one was held in 1921[N]
- **Thingwall** Mill, built in 1866, was sold and later demolished
- The nine acre site for the Royal Liverpool Children's Hospital in Telegraph Road **Heswall** was purchased for £2,500 [see 1905][YW6]
- The manse for the **Neston** Presbyterian Church was erected next to the church in Parkgate Road[YW6]

Jul 10   Shop, smithy and 3 cottages **Irby** sold at auction £500[LCPSR]

Aug 22   *The Gables* **Barnston** sold at auction £1,000[LCPSR]

Nov   Lychgate erected at St Bartholomew's Church **Thurstaston** by Margaret Ismay in memory of her late husband Thomas Ismay[TIL]

Above: *John Wilson is seen on the left with his delivery horse and cart. The business operated from his shop at the corner of Pensby Road and Telegraph Road **Heswall** until about 1909 when it was taken over by W Kelly who also ran it as a bakery [see advert below]*

Below: *The advert is for John Wilson who would deliver sacks of flour in one of their 'vans' - one of which is seen above. When John Wilson sold the business to W Kelly it included the 'vans' and Mr Kelly replaced J Wilson's name with his own*

Above: *Bishop Wilson's School, which was founded in c.1724, is pictured in **Burton**. The school moved to new premises in 1963 and the building is now a private residence*

Below: *Saughall Tower Mill is pictured with its sails in tact - it was last operated in 1926, then fell into a state of disrepair. It was renovated much later and is now a private house [see 1909]*

Above: *The Durham Ox is pictured in **Little Neston**. It dated back as a beerhouse to at least 1889 when there were two beerhouses and three fully licenced houses mentioned in Sulley's The Hundred of Wirral. It still stands overlooking the Village Green and is now two private houses*

1901

- The Vicarage was built in Parkgate Road **Neston**[N]
- The thatched *Old Royal Oak Inn* **Little Neston** burnt down and replaced with a new building behind the old one [see photo page 32][N]

May 14 *Hawthorne Cottage* Wadescroft **Thingwall** sold at auction £300[LCPSR]

Jun 24 *Conway Cottage* Thurstaston Road **Heswall** sold at auction £1,000[LCPSR]

Sep 28 Shop and bakehouse **Little Neston** sold at auction £360[LCPSR]

Population at 1901 Census - compared with 1891:

	1891	1901
Barnston	404	522
Birkenhead	58,287	110,915**
Burton	266	222
Gayton	199	180
Heswall-cum-Oldfield	1,210	2,167
Irby	174	146
Leighton	325	728
Ness	354	355
Neston-cum-Parkgate	–	4,154*
Neston - Great	2,240	2,201
Neston - Little	1,012	–
Pensby	51	48
Puddington	150	126
Shotwick	77	82
Shotwick Park	8	8
Thingwall	173	156
Thurstaston	145	141

**Birkenhead Borough boundaries extended
*Parkgate was created out of Great Neston and Leighton[TGW]

Above: These wooden steps were the main point of access to the beach from the south end of The Parade at **Parkgate***. Mostyn House School is the tall building above the base of the steps, with the small rounded building to the right being the school's covered playground which was erected in 1891*[N]

Above: The sign for J Johnson - 'Plumber, Decorative House and Sign Painter' is seen in High Street **Neston**

Above: The pony has just hauled the water cart up the hill in Hill Bark Road from a well at the bottom and is heading towards Mill Hill Road **Irby**

Above: The house between the girls on the right and the horses in **Barnston Village** *served teas*

Below left: Behind the two men on the wall used to stand **Irby** *Windmill [see 1896]. The* Miller's Cottage *beyond was in Mill Lane and now forms part of* The Mill *pub*

– **Burton** *Manor* purchased by Henry Neville Gladstone, third son of WE Gladstone - the former Prime Minister[BIW]

– **Neston** Liberal Club opened in Liverpool Road **Neston** - cost £3,000 - renamed Neston Institute in 1908 - later known as the Civic Hall

Hotel Victoria opened in Gayton Road **Lower Heswall** [see 1908] - took the licence from the *White Lion* at the junction of Wall Rake and Gayton Road [see photo next page and 1937]

– The second **Neston** Telephone exchange opened in the front room of a cottage in Liverpool Road [see 1926 text]

– **Neston** sewage works was built

– Local architect Aubrey Thomas, who designed the Liver Building in **Liverpool** and was a Dickensian addict, who named all seven daughters after Dickens' characters and called his new house on The Parade **Parkgate** *Bleak House* - it was later called *Brooke House*

May 28 *The New Farm* **Neston** 102 acres sold at auction in four lots £6,800[LCPSR]

Jun 11 *Beechfield* and cottage **Barnston** withdrawn at auction at £1,400 - reserve £1,550[LCPSR]

Jun 26 Coronation Day for King Edward VII and Queen Alexandra[SOUV]

Jul 26 *Moorside House* + 2 acres Parkgate Road **Neston** sold at auction £1,200 and Moorside Field 3 acres £300[LCPSR]

Sep 6 Informal opening of the new nine hole **Heswall** Golf Club [see 1909][HGC]

Sep 11 The Hallfield Brickworks Burton Road and Colliery Road **Neston** over 5 acres sold at auction £1,000[LCPSR]

Oct 20 **Heswall** Consumption Hospital opened[YW6]

Dec White Star Line, founded by the late Thomas Ismay of *Dawpool* **Thurstaston**, was taken over by the American financier JP Morgan [it was said that if Thomas Ismay had been alive the sale would never have taken place]

Above: Pear Tree Cottage - *formerly* Pear Tree Farm **Burton** *had a datestone 'JLSL 1682' which probably referred to John Leather and his wife Sarah. At one time it had over 30 acres of land. The entrance can be seen to the rear of the house and barn behind*[BIW]

Above: Burton *Mill, whose entrance on the right is partly hidden by the ivy, is seen here reduced to its brick base and part of its central wooden structure. However, it looks much safer than some 17 years previously [see 1885]*

TELEPHONE No. 25.

G. REDDY,

FAMILY BUTCHER,

Heswall Hill.

PURVEYOR OF PRIMEST ENGLISH MEAT.

Established 1863.

Left: Irby *Village Post Office on the right was then the only shop in the village with Mrs Leech as the Postmistress - her husband Horatio was described as a joiner, wheelwright and undertaker. The road had been improved and a pavement added since the turn of the century [see 1899]*

Above: *The* Farmer's Arms *is seen on the Chester High Road at* **Leighton**, *which once stood opposite Boathouse Lane. This West Cheshire Brewery inn was withdrawn at auction [see 1907], but the interesting detail was that it was mentioned as the "late Rose and Thistle". It had lost its licence by 1922 and then traded as refreshment rooms. The building was an odd shape with only three quarters built - the missing quarter can be seen with no sloping roof top right. The building was demolished with the site becoming a small industrial estate including Darlingtons and a garage with showroom*[YW6]

Above: *Looking along Telegraph Road towards* **Heswall** *Cross with the signpost on the right pointing towards* **Barnston**. *Fox's Hardware and Household Requisite shop was the first shop pictured on the right [see below]*

Below: *An advert for Fox's shop which is seen in the photograph above to the right of the signpost*

THE PRIORY SCHOOL.
NESTON. CHESHIRE.

Above: *The Priory School is the tall building in Park Street viewed from the top of Buggen Lane* **Neston**. *There were several girls' schools here from 1813 until the 1890s when it became the Priory School [boys] until about 1910. The eight acre site with its own water supply was later sold and the telephone exchange built here*[N]

Above: *The sign for Gayton Road is seen above the doorway of the old* White Lion *which stood at the bottom of Wall Rake* **Lower Heswall**. *It is said that the licence was passed to the new* Hotel Victoria *in 1902. The building pictured is still there today as* White Lodge[YW6]

Right: *Gayton Mill is seen in a ruinous state with wooden parts of the mill stacked up in the doorway behind the lady and window frames on her left [see 1894]*

1903

  —   New vicarage bought for **Neston** Parish Church in Parkgate Road[N]

May 27 *Thistlefield House* Irby Lane **Heswall** sold at auction £1,250[LCPSR]

Aug 2   1st Worcester RGA [Volunteers] arrived at **Parkgate** by train for their annual camp [see photo below]

Sep 23 Oldfield Common [part] **Heswall** - over 3 acres sold at auction £72. 10 shillings - also over 21 acres land on The Dale **Heswall** £1,800[LCPSR]

Above: *The rebuilt* Royal Oak *is seen from the Village Green* **Little Neston** *with the signs on the gates either side advertising its owner Birkenhead Brewery [see 1893]*

Above: *The delapidated buildings on the left faced Mostyn Square* **Parkgate** *[named after the family who owned all the village from 1672 to 1849]*

Right: *Local people have gathered to watch and listen to the band of the 1st Worcester RGA [volunteers]. They were marching down the slope from* **Parkgate** *Station, their train is still seen on the platform, leading the men to their camp on Parks Field - some of their tents at the camp can be seen in the background. There was an artillery range nearby on the marshes which was the reason for the camps here before the First World War*

Left: *This rural scene taken in Burton Road* **Ness** *shows the only shop in the village - the thatched building on the left whose goods can be seen in the first window - which was run by Edith Roberts. The main business in the village was Mealor & Sons, whose sign can be seen above their works [see advert 1915]*

Left: *The lady is waiting with her horse and carriage by the Smithy in The Village **Burton**. The blacksmith at the time was Samuel Henshaw, who was also a wheelwright. The smithy has long gone but the two cottages in the background are still there today*

Below: Backwood Hall *Boathouse Lane **Parkgate**, was pictured on a postcard in 1903. It was described as a small mansion, built in red brick in Flemish bond with slate roof, in Jacobean style. In a directory of 1850 it was described as "... it commands a delightful view of the Dee, and is the seat of Hugh Craig Esq. By 1871 Theodore Rathbone was in residence. Backwood Hall is a Grade II listed building and can be seen from the Wirral Way - annual events are organised in the grounds*

Above: *To the left of the lady with the delivery cart and wicker baskets is a post boy with a bicycle seen in Village Road **Lower Heswall**. He is standing at the bottom of the steps wich led up to the single-storey Post Office [just out of sight] which had been erected in 1899. Note the cobbled pavements and the lady whose long white dress must have picked up dirt from the road including horse droppings - especially when it rained!*

Right: *The bunting and flags are out for the Chester to Parkgate Race 24 June 1903 [either running or cycle] with the crowd awaiting the winner. The licensee of the Birkenhead Brewery pub the Chester Hotel **Parkgate**, seen behind the crowd, was WT Sleddon. The postcard says that the lady holding the boy to the right of the horse and carriage was probably Mrs Bushell and her son Tom*

1904

– There were nine licensed houses within 320yds. of **Neston** Cross[N]

– **Heswall** Golf Club erected their first clubhouse at a cost of £1,571 [see photo page 37][HGC]

– *Puddington Hall* built

Jul 20 Shop and bakehouse, Telegraph Road **Heswall** sold at auction £805[LCPSR]

Sep 28 *Poplar Cottage* **Greasby** sold at auction £550 - also The Slack, Slack Road, 5 cottages £500 - also *Oaklands Farm* **Heswall, Barnston** and **Pensby** comprising farmhouse, *Glenburnie Lodge*, 6 cottages and 123 acres of land £8,500[LCP]

Oct 15 *Rookery Farm* **Irby** 78 acres sold £4,625[LCPSR]

Nov 21 A mission and young men's club opened at Gills Lane **Pensby** - attached to Christ Church **Barnston**[KD]

*Above: This local man is looking at what was known as the 'Quakers' Graves' which were in the woods behind **Burton** Church. These were deliberate burials outside consecrated ground although the stones were not in Quaker style. There have been several explanations but none convincing - this is one of Wirral's mysterys!*

*Above: These two timber-framed cottages were examples of the early houses in **Burton**. The boys on the right are standing under the sign for 'JH Suckley - Licenced to Sell Tobacco - Cycles Stored'. The cottages were owned by the Hospital of St John Lichfield who sold them in 1955 and they were converted into one house[BW]*

*Above: Moorland House School is seen on the horizon in Hillside Road **Heswall**. It was founded by Mr L Dobie in the early 1900s. During the Second World War the school moved to North Wales and the building housed evacuees from **Wallasey** and **Liverpool**. The school was demolished in the early 1970s and houses built on the site. Dawstone Road is seen bottom centre and part of the smithy on the extreme left [see 1931]*

Above: *The photographer has told the children, who are in their 'Sunday best', to run towards him on the sands at **Parkgate** with Mostyn Square in the background to the left of the last four children on the right*

Above: *The **Neston** Liberal Club in Hinderton Road, which was built in 1901/02 at a cost of £3,000, could accommodate 900 people. Facilities included: billiards; smoking and reading room; baths and lavatories. A verandah is seen on the right overlooked the bowling green and there were also two tennis courts. In 1908 it was renamed the Neston Institute and in 1914 became a Red Cross hospital [see 1915]*

Above: Sunnybank Cottage, *which can be seen built into the sandstone, stood opposite* Church Farm **Burton**

Above: *The caption on this postcard says:* 'Friendship Farm, **Burton** Woods, Cheshire'. *It was described as being part of the **Ness** Estate with over 13 acres and was sold at auction 21 July 1896 for £570 - also part of the estate was* Haddon Hall Farm *which had 206 acres sold for £6,025 and 16 lots of land for £5,000[LCPSR]*

W Smallwood
COAL MERCHANT
THE VILLAGE HESWALL

Above: *This was a postcard of the Mostyn House School 'rifle range' on the sands at **Parkgate** with the school in the background on the Parade. The postcard was sent by the headmaster Hon. Capt. AG Grenfell [probably the master with the pipe] to a local regiment challenging them to a shooting match: "The Cadet Corps [60 boys] would be glad to shoot a match, with carbines, 10 a side, 10 shots [3 sighters & 7 to count] at each range of 100 yds. and 200 yds., against the officers of the regiment any afternoon in June or July when the tides are 'neap' - 26 March 1904"*

- **Neston** Concord Society formed - staged Gilbert and Sullivan operas - renamed the Neston Amateur Operatic Society in 1920. They gave their last performance in 1955[N]
- **Neston** cemetery formed in Raby Park Road - 2.5 acres cost £3,600 - first grave dated 1907[KD]
- The following public houses lost their license:- *Sawyer's Arms* **Parkgate**; *Golden Lion* and *Nag's Head* **Neston**[N]

Feb 8 *Heather Brow* The Mount **Heswall** sold at auction £410 and *Campion's Head* or *Turf Tavern* corner Market Square **Parkgate** sold at auction £440[LCPSR]

Apr 21 The foundation stone laid for the Liverpool Children's Hospital Telegraph Road **Heswall** [see 1915][RLCHCH]

Above: *This postcard of* **Gayton** *sent in 1905 was said to be* Rose Farm, *a sandstone cottage in Gayton Lane*

Above: *This 1905 postcard was entitled 'Bee's Gardens'. The house pictured was* Mickwell Brow *built for Arthur Bulley in 1898 on a sandstone outcrop which had previously been used as a public open space. Soon the surrounding area and farm fields were converted into ornamental gardens including herbaceous borders, a large plant propogation area, fruit and vegetable section and a rock and water garden. A commercial nursery was founded here in 1904 and after became Bees Seeds. In 1911 they moved to a 1,000 acre site at Sealand*[NG]

Above: *The three ladies are standing outside* Stanley House *in* **Burton**. *This was originally the* Stanley Arms *- one of five alehouses in Burton in 1561 when it was the port for* **Chester**. *By 1850 this was one of two and in 1860 there were no licensed premises listed [see 1919]*[BIW]

Left: *Manor Farm was built c.1640 in Thingwall Road* **Irby** *[see 1912] the Anchor Inn is left of the farmhouse*

Left: *Heswall Station looking towards* **Thurstaston** *with the Station Master's house between the two canopies by the bridge in Station Road [see 1926]*

Above: *Looking towards the Villge Green* **Little Neston** *from the* Royal Oak, *there was a large boulder in front of the inn. This was found in a field off Badger Bait. The council about 1930 wanted to break it up for road mending purposes. However, Lord Leverhulme did a swap - supplying all the road material in exchange for the stone, which is now a permanent fixture in* Thornton Manor *gardens and has a fountain on it[YW6]*

Above: *Families of the fishermen are waiting with their horse and carts to unload their catch at* **Parkgate.** Dee Cottages *on The Parade are seen on the right*

Above: *Neston Parish Church of St Mary and St Helen was the second church to be built on this site. The original was probably of Saxon date replaced in the 12th century, with this present one being rebuilt in 1875. Emily Lyon was baptised here 12 May 1765 [see 1865]*

Above: *Neston Presbyterian Church is seen in Parkgate Road on the corner of Moorside Lane. The church was founded in* **Parkgate** *in 1857 moving here when this building opened 18 July 1884 [the Parkgate church later became St Thomas's Church]. The Manse was built in 1900 and the church later became the Parkgate and Neston United Reformed Church in 1972 [see 1909]*

Above: *Heswall Golf Club was founded in 1902 overlooking the River Dee on land leased from John Baskerville Glegg. Worked commenced on the nine hole course in June and was ready for the informal opening by 1 September 1902. The temporary clubhouse was part of* Gayton Hall Farm *[see 1907] and with a membership of almost 200, the club was able to build a new clubhouse next to the temporary one, opening in 1904. This two-storied wooden clubhouse was unfortunately burnt down 20 January 1924. Although the manager of the* Hotel Victoria *was informed and summoned the* **Birkenhead** *Fire Brigade, the pitch pine building was burnt down, together with some farm outbuildings - total damage estimated at £10,000. The new clubhouse opened June 1926[HGC]*

Above: *Mr Bushell, seen with his daughter, was a* **Parkgate** *fisherman. He normally wore shoes or wellingtons but was asked by the photographer to go barefoot!*

1906

- Mostyn House School **Parkgate** built a water tower which was fed from their well
- Mostyn House School **Parkgate** had become just a preparatory school up to the age of 13[N]
- A Village Hall was erected in **Burton**, paid for by HN Gladstone [see 1933][KD]
- The purpose-built Telephone Exchange, which had moved from Bank Buildings, opened in The Mount **Heswall** - there were then 74 subscribers

Jan 27   Dawpool National School opened at **Thurstaston** [see photo next page][YW6]

Mar 2   *Nag's Head* ph. **Neston** sold at auction [licence extinguished] £575 - also late *Sawyers Arms Inn* The Parade **Parkgate** £500[LCPSR]

Mar 27   *Laburnum Cottages* [two] Irby Lane **Heswall** sold at Auction £270[LCPSR]

Apr 10   *The Old Brewery Buildings* High Street / Chester Road **Neston** sold at auction £500 - also *The Old Quay House* + 22 acres adjoining land £1,050 + land adjacent, front River Dee 2 acres £115[LCPSR]

Jun   Bees Limited set up by Arthur K Bulley at **Ness**[N]

Oct 27   *Shotwick Park* 1,328 acres sold at auction £70,000 - also *Shotwick House Farm* 41.5 acres sold £2,250[LCPSR]

Above: Birch Bros. *fruiterers and florists shop at 31 The Mount* **Heswall** *is today a private house. Note Heswall Castle on the left [see below]*

Above: **Heswall** Castle, *which was built on land between The Mount and Telegraph Road, became a home for the Female Orphan Society [see 1915]*

Above: Ashfield Hall *stood on the west side of the Chester High Road near its junction with Liverpool Road* **Neston.** *The hall is now a one storey building with windows blocked off, converted into a grain store [see page 5]*

Above: This picture postcard was posted in 1906 and shows one of the first cars in Telegraph Road **Heswall**

Above: Some of the machinery and workings are seen at the Wirral colliery. **Little Neston** *By 1892 the Wirral Colliery Company had taken over and were mining 100,000 tons of coal a year with workings which extended over 1.75 miles under the Dee*

Neston's *first May Queen 1906*

Above: *The newly-built Dawpool National School is seen in School Lane* **Thurstaston** *shortly after it opened 27 January 1906 with 112 children. It was built for Margaret Ismay, in memory of her husband Thomas*

Above right: *The water tower built at Mostyn House School* **Parkgate** *in 1906, was so designed that it looked nothing like a water tower, but blended in with the other buildings and was pleasing to the eye [see 1918]*

Above: *Over 100 years ago this was a popular cafe for cyclists, being at a main junction for roads from* **Chester** *to* **Heswall** *and* **Birkenhead** *to Wales [to the right]. There were no give-way signs then due to lack of traffic. Today it is now known as the 'Two Mills' or 'Welsh crossroads' [see 1953]. The cast iron mile post on the right was erected in 1896. The telegraph poles, which disappear into the distance must have been 30ft. to 40ft. high*

Above: *The Bushell Drinking Fountain was erected in* **Neston** *1882 using the well that Christopher Bushell had sunk. Jackson's Tower behind was erected by George Jackson whose chemist shop was next door. This was a folly with no useful purpose other than giving the owner good views over the Dee to Wales*

Above: *The crowds are watching the annual* **Neston** *Ladies' Day procession, on the first Thursday in June, which is proceeding down the High Street in front of the* Brown Horse Inn *at the junction of Bridge Street [see 1914]*

Right: *This seems to be the gathering place for people of* **Parkgate** *- by the side of the old* Watch House *[see 1880]. The newly-built* Bleak House *- later known as* Brook House *can be see to the left. This was built c.1904 for W Aubrey Thomas, the architect of the* Liver Building

1907

– Work started on the Akbar Nautical School in Greenfield Lane **Heswall** at a cost of over £17,000 - it moved here from its ship of the same name berthed off **New Ferry**

Mar 7 Land - 1,136 sq. yds. on corner of Telegraph Road and The Mount **Heswall** including *Laurel* and *Saltbox* cottages sold at auction 13 shillings sq. yd.[LCPSR]

Apr 9 Margaret Ismay of *Dawpool* **Thurstaston**, wife of Thomas Ismay, died[TH]

Jul 1 *Bankside* and *Dawley Cottage*, Hillside Road **Heswall** sold at auction £480[LCPSR]

Sep 27 *Farmer's Arms* bh. [late *Rose and Thistle*] Chester Road **Leighton**, **Neston** withdrawn at auction £1,025 - reserve £1,200[LCPSR]

Above: *The horse and carriage is outside the* Chester Hotel *in Station Road* **Parkgate**. *The inn dated back to the 1850s with John Acton the victualler in 1874 when it was also the Posting House [see 1960]*

Right: *These girls are posing for the photographer Arthur Maycock of Parkgate [many of his photographs were sold as postcards before the First World War - which helped to record what life was like then] either on or besides a boat beached at* **Parkgate** *with the* Watch House *seen right background*

Below: *Looking along Moorside Lane* **Neston** *- Old Quay Lane is on the right, Moorside Avenue is seen on the left opposite* Moor End House *and the building in the distance is the Neston Presbyterian Church [see 1905]. Parkside Close is now on the left*

Below: *St Bartholomew's Church* **Thurstaston** *pictured here was the third church at Thurstaston, built in memory of Joseph Hegan by his daughters at a cost of £6,000 - consecrated in 1886[YW6]*

Left: Gayton Hall Farm, *Gayton Lane* **Gayton** *was used as a temporary clubhouse by* **Heswall Golf Club** *when it opened in 1902 until the clubhouse was built next to it in 1904 - part of the clubhouse is seen on the extreme left [see 1909]*

Below: *The Cleaver Sanitorium [West Derby Union Hospital] was opened off Oldfield Road **Heswall** in 1902. It was a brick building with 50 beds and from 1913 was used for children only. This photograph shows the original building before an extension either side. In 1939, the children were evacuated to **Rhuddlan** and adult patients were then admitted. In 1950 it changed its name to Cleaver Hospital. By 1988 it had closed and the land sold*

Above: *This was **Heswall** AFC's second ground Church Meadow off Farr Hall Road, where they moved in 1906, using a nearby mortuary as a changing room. They moved at one time to a pitch on the 'Puddydale', opposite the Royal Children's Hospital, Telegraph Road [seen left horizon], and were known as the 'Puddies' or 'Puddydalians'. The double-fronted house on the left in Delavor Road, opposite Farr Hall Road, is today* Tarbert House *on the left and* Lullingfields *on the right.* Heswall Castle *can be seen above the goal post*[HAFC]

Above: *This postcard which celebrated the centenary of the Wesleyan Chapel Telegraph Road **Heswall** showed the interior of the church on the left and exterior on the right. The church, which was opposite the Police Station, was built of local red sandstone. It was erected in 1891 in the late decorated style at a cost of £1,450 and seated 350. An organ was added in 1909*[KD]

Above: *The caption on this postcard said 'The Junior **Heswall** Club 1907'*

Above: *St Winefride Roman Catholic Church was erected as a school in 1840, being built as a neat Gothic stone structure, designed by AWN Pugin. It was adapted as a chapel in 1843, when the Presbytery was enlarged. It replaced a chapel in **Puddington** Hall once used by Roman Catholics - as described in a stain glass window in the church, commemorating Father Plessington, who was executed as a traitor in the 17th century. As the congregation increased, further extensions were required in 1852 which provided a further 100 seats. The adjacent school and teacher's house were built in 1856*

1908

– **Chester** Co-op Society opened a branch in **Neston** on the site of the *Golden Lion Hotel* - selling groceries, clothes and shoes[N]

Jan **Neston** Library opened in Parkgate Road - [see photo][N]

Jun 27 Foundation stone laid for the Wesleyan Church **Neston** [see photo]

Jul 12 4th Lancashire RFA arrived at **Parkgate** for their annual camp [see photo]

Above: *TL Dobbs speaking at the laying of foundation stones for the Wesleyan Church at the junction of High Street and Park Street [to the left] Neston 27 June 1908*

Above: *This fine looking sandstone building was erected as Lloyd's Bank c.1904 at the junction of Telegraph Road and The Mount Heswall [to the right], replacing an old cottage. For many years this building has caused a bottle-neck in Heswall, but all attempts to have it demolished or moved have failed[YW6]*

Above: *A croquet lawn is seen in this rear view of Hotel Victoria in Lower Heswall*

Above: *The 4th Lancashire RFA heading towards the Parks Field 12 July 1908 arrived by train at Parkgate Station [in Parkgate Road off to the right]. The horse-drawn Royal Field Artillery was responsible for the medium calibre guns and howitzers and the sands at Parkgate were ideal for firing practice. The Neston Parish vicarage is seen to the left beyond Earl Drive [see photo below]*

Above: *The entrance to Neston Library is seen in Parkgate Road Neston. It was built on land donated in memory of Dr Russell and £1,200 was provided towards the cost by Andrew Carnegie - it opened December 1908[YW6]*

Above: *Neston Mill is in the background in Leighton Road Neston behind the cows. Taken from Parkgate Road the road to the left was Earl Drive built in 1903 and named after the developer NA Earl. The sign in the field pictured in the photo above this one was for the development in Leighton Park Estate, which was in Earl Drive. However, no Leighton Park ever existed - it was a name invented by the developer![YW6]*

1909

- Council school opened in new premises in Burton Road **Neston**[N]
- Christ Church Baptist Mission Chapel opened near Wirral Colliery **Little Neston** for the use of the colliers and their families. It is now the site of a house in Quayside[YWPH]
- First Official Scout camp ever was held at Irby Hill [Dodd's] Farm Irby Hill Road **Irby**[YW6]

Jan 30 Heswall Sailing Club formed at a meeting in the *Hotel Victoria* **Heswall** - its name was changed to the Dee Sailing Club in 1912[SOUV]

Feb 15 Part of the Liverpool Children's Hospital Telegraph Road **Heswall** was ready for its first patients[RLCHCH]

Apr 15 Opening service for newly-built **Heswall** Presbyterian Church of England Telegraph Road[YWPH]

May 1 **Caldy** Station opened on the **Hooton** to **West Kirby** railway line[RSW]

Sep 3 The *Akbar* Nautical Training School opened at **Heswall** in 10 acres of ground - cost £17,000[YW]

Oct 8 **Heswall** Council Mixed School officially opened[TSP]

*Above: Looking across the fields and golf course towards the original **Heswall** Golf Clubhouse on the left and Gayton Hall Farm next door to the right [see 1905 & 1907]*

*Above: Mr Esther is seen standing proudly in front of the horse-drawn delivery van for Esther & Co Family Baker of Poll Hill **Heswall***

*Above: Originally called the Hinderton Inn on the Chester High Road, at the junction with Hinderton Road **Neston**, it had been called the Shrewsbury Arms since at least 1850 when the victualler was Moses Robinson, who was also a veterinary surgeon - it is now known as the Hinderton Arms*

*Above: Looking down towards the Dee View from the top of The Mount **Heswall** - the cyclist is just on the bend*

*Above: This group of Wesleyan Band of Hope Workers **Parkgate** [no alcohol permitted] were attached to the Wesleyan church and preached the evils of alcohol [see 1905]. **Neston** and Parkgate had a serious problem due to the high number of pubs*

*Above: Looking along Thingwall Road towards **Irby** village [see Vine Cottage 1912]*

Above: *A pathway has been cleared for pedestrians through the snow on The Parade **Parkgate** with the road still mostly covered in snow. Mostyn House School is on the right with the* Union Hotel *[later the* Ship Hotel*] behind the cart and the building beyond was* Dee House *which was replaced with Nicholls' 'ice cream' parlour and cafe'*

WIRRAL RAILWAY.

New Saturday Afternoon Excursion

BY THROUGH TRAIN.

Commencing JULY 17th, 1909, and **EVERY SATURDAY**
During JULY, AUGUST, and SEPTEMBER (unless previously withdrawn)

CHEAP EXCURSION TICKETS

will be issued from the Wirral Railway Co's Stations shown below :

To CALDY, THURSTASTON, HESWALL & PARKGATE

(Via WEST KIRBY)

FROM	Times of Starting	RETURN FARE SAME DAY 3rd Class			
		To CALDY	To THURSTON	To HESWALL	To PARKGATE
	p.m.				
SEACOMBE & EGREMONT	2·45	1/1	1/1	1/1	1/1
Liscard and Poulton	2 49	11	11	11	11
Moreton	2 57	11	11	11	1·1
Meols	3 1	—	—	11	11
HOYLAKE	3 5	—	—	—	11
‡NEW BRIGHTON	2 30	11	11	11	11
‡Wallasey	2 33	11	11	11	11
‡Wallasey Village	2 35	11	11	11	11
‡BIRKENHEAD, Docks	2 55	11	11	11	11
‡BIRKENHEAD, Park	2 52	11	11	11	11

N.B.—The Boat connecting with this Excursion Train leaves Liverpool Landing Stage at 2·30 p.m.

Passengers marked ‡ CHANGE TRAINS at West Kirby.

Passengers RETURN the same day only, as under :—	
FROM	FOR ALL STATIONS
Parkgate	8-43 p.m.
Heswall	8-48 p.m.
Thurstaston	8-54 p.m.
Caldy	8-58 p.m.

Children under 3 free ; above 3 and under 12 years of age half-fares.   No Luggage allowed.

Excursion Tickets are only available to and from the Stations named upon them, and any Passenger using them on the Outward or Return Journey at any Station short of, or beyond the Stations named upon them, or travelling by any other train than those mentioned on the Excursion bills, will forfeit the Ticket, and will be charged the Ordinary Fare. The contract and liability of such Company or Proprietor are limited to their own Railway, Coaches or Steamboats, and their Tickets are issued subject to the conditions and regulations referred to in the Time Tables, Books, Bills, and Notices of the respective Companies and Proprietors on whose Railways, Coaches, or Steamboats such Tickets are available.

All information regarding Excursion Bookings, Pleasure Parties, Special Trains, Time Tables and Illustrated Guides, &c., can be obtained on application to

NEW BRIGHTON, July, 1909.   Telephone 64 Liscard.   **J. H. BURNS,** *Traffic Manager.*

Above: *This was a poster for the Wirral Railway 'Saturday Afternoon Cheap Excursion' including to **Thurstaston**, **Heswall** and **Parkgate** from all parts of Wirral. One stipulation was 'no luggage allowed'*

Above: *This was a horse called 'Handy' clearing the first fence in the Wirral Hunt Point to Point heavy weight competition. **Saughall** Mill is in the background [see 1900]*

Below: *Looking across the Old Quay Fields at **Neston** towards the River Dee. The buildings in the distance to the right were originally Dee Side Electric Works [see 1882]. In 1896 the Neston and **Parkgate** Hygenic Laundry and Cleaning Co was formed here, closing in the late 1950s*

Above: *Old Vicarage **Neston** stood on the corner of High Street and Bridge Street - today there is a supermarket on the site*

Above: *The local children are enjoying a paddle in the River Dee with a slag heap from Wirral Colliery **Little Neston** coal mine behind, together with some of the colliery buildings [see 1927]*

1910

- The **Parkgate** Chapel in Mostyn Square was leased by the Church of England who purchased the building seven years later, naming it after Saint Thomas
- There were allegations in the magazine *John Bull* of abuse at the Reformatory Akbar Nautical Training School, Heswall. They were rejected, but found that there had been instances of 'irregular punishments'

Jan 29   The Liverpool Children's Hospital Telegraph Road **Heswall** received the 'Royal' prefix from HRH Edward VII[RLCHCH]

Above: The Old Harp Inn, *which faced the River Dee at* **Ness**, *was mentioned in ale licences records from the 1790s. In 1828 when it was known as* The Welch Harp *Robert Robinson the licensee. Its main trade came from the nearby colliery which operated on and off from 1760 until 1927 [see 1960]*

Above: *Behind the hedge on the left was the main road leading up to what was known as the* **Thurstaston** *cutting. This was constructed at the expense of Thomas Ismay, founder of the White Star Line. The reason for that was the road pictured was the original main road from* **West Kirby** *to* **Heswall** *and continued past the front of his house Dawpool. As he did not want to be disturbed by the noise he paid for the road to be diverted and this became a private road [see 1887]*

Above: *This was a picture postcard with the address Gayton Cottage* **Heswall** *Cheshire embossed on it - which was the house in the background. The message said "This is where I live. The man is carrying some ducks from the punt, yours Peg". A ferry service was used from* Gayton Cottage *to North Wales before 1820*

Above: *The writing on the chalk board at the front said:* '*Parkgate CE Infants' School 1910'. Miss Catherine Norman is the teacher on the back row and Miss Theresa Mealor the Headmistress on the front row*

Above: *This was* Kemp's Cottage **Heswall** *named after the local roadman who lived here. To the left of the cottage is a small white hut which was the 'outside loo'. The cottage was demolished c.1912*

Left: *Thurstaston Station was opened in 1886 on the* **Hooton** *to* **West Kirby** *line. Originally it was to be built further inland but Thomas Ismay, who was Chairman of the railway company, did not want the line close to his house Dawpool, so it was re-routed. The line was closed to passengers in 1956 and to goods 1962. The track was taken up and now forms the Wirral Way - the Visitor Centre was opened at Thurstaston in 1973 on a site towards the shore and to the left of the men*

1910 continued

Right: *There must have been a popular event at the south end of the Parade at **Parkgate** - as there are at least two cars and several horses and carriages, together with a crowd gathered in a group*

Below: *The house and yard belonging to Mr P Bridson is seen fronting onto Bridge Street **Neston**. His business was described as 'Steam Threshing & Saw Mill Proprietor, Manufacturer and dealer in Bone Manures, Steam Ploughing etc'*

Left: *This early steam-driven threshing machine at Hillside Farm Dawstone Road **Heswall** was sent as a postcard in 1910. The farmhouse building is still there today*

Above: White House Farm *in **Puddington** had a datestone seen above the porch of 1710. The building is still there today without the steps and porch and is known just as* White House

Left: *This was the summer camp for the Maitland Mission of Oxton Boys Brigade at a farm in **Pensby** - their band is seated at the front performing for the photographer. Their non-denominational corrugated iron Mission Hall was in Newlands Lane to the rear of the* Queens Arms **Oxton**. *They moved to new premises in Storeton Road in 1929*

1911

- The Wirral Colliery Company at **Little Neston** Colliery went bankrupt[N]
- Bees Seeds moved from **Ness** to a 1,000 acre at **Sealand** [see 1905][YW6]

Jun 22 Coronation of King George V and Queen Mary [see Brewer's Arms and school photos]

Jul 22 There was a 'great' fire reported in *Dawpool* grounds [see photo]

Above: The Brewer's Arms *in High Street* **Neston** *is decorated with flags, bunting and photographs for the Coronation of King George V and Queen Mary on 22 June 1911. The inn had a datestone of 1670 - the victualler in 1828 was Wm. Hughes and in 1874 it was George Hall who was also a joiner. The children were all dressed up for the special day with two of the boys wearing Coronation medals. However, the girl on the right is content to play with her hoop*

Above: *The cows are meandering along Leighton Road* **Neston***, passing Neston Mill. This was built mid 18th century of tower construction and was last used in the 1880s. Originally there were two mills but one was destroyed c.1828*

Right: *The caption on this postcard read 'The great fire in* Dawpool *grounds 22 July 1911' [see below]*

Below: *This imposing building* Dawpool **Thurstaston** *was the home of the Ismay family, owners of the White Star Line. The original* Dawpool *was built here in 1865 by James Hegan. The 390 acre site was bought by Thomas Ismay in 1877 and having demolished the old building, this new one was erected in 1884*

Right: *This group photograph of the* **Heswall** *Council School was taken on King George V's Coronation Day 22 June 1911 with many of the children wearing their Coronation medal. Otherwise known as the 'Puddydale' School, it was opened 11 October 1909. It closed in 1982 and the site is now occupied by flats [see 1954][YW6]*

Above: *The children are posing for the photographer in Pensby Road* **Pensby**. *Gills Lane is in the distance to the right behind the children*

Above: *Sir Wilfred T Grenfell was born at Mostyn House School* **Parkgate** *28 February 1865, where his parents ran the school. He had established the Labrador Medical Mission in 1893 and in over 40 years he had built up an organisation that included six hospitals, seven nursing stations, four hospital ships, four boarding schools, 14 industrial centres, 12 clothing distribution centres, a co-operative lumber mill, and a seaman's institute at St Johns Newfoundland. He died in 1940*

Above: *This was an advertising postcard for Nicholson High Street* **Neston** *who were drapers and outfitters. Their shop can be seen on the left taken from the church*

Above: *The men outside* **Lower Heswall** *smithy were said to be from the left: Billy Barlow, Sam Hough, Vernon and Mr Shone - the horse had a cover which said 'Sam Hough Oldfield Farm Heswall'*

Above: *This group of people are posing for the photographer in* **Barnston** *Village. The shop and Post Office is to the left and Storeton Lane to the right*

Left: *The three boys with the water cart being pulled by a donkey have stopped by the farmyard entrance to* Irby Hill Farm, *in Mill Hill Road* **Irby** *[see 1887]. The boys, who were surrounded by hens [definitely 'free range'], had been down to collect water from the well at the bottom of Hill Bark Road*

1912

- Films first shown at **Neston** by the Neston Electric Picturedrome Company - at the Institute Hinderton Road[TSSW]
- John Cameron opened a shop and workshop near The Cross in **Neston** where he sold and repaired motor cars and cycles. In 1916 he was called up and because of his skills, served as an engineer in the Royal Flying Corps - his wife carried on the business[N]
- Kings Hall built in Telegraph Road **Heswall** - later to become a bus depot [see 1921] and then a cinema [see 1950][TSSW]
- Jul 16 Mr King flew his biplane from **Freshfield** and landed on the sand at **Parkgate -** to show his plane to the Mostyn House School boys [see photo][N]

Above: *This was the rear view of* St Nicholas House **Burton**, with Church House *to the right. This was the official vicarage in the 19th century until it was replaced in 1911 by one built in Vicarage Lane at the expense of Henry Neville Gladstone of* Burton Manor *[see 1913]*

Left: Manor Farm *on the corner of Thingwall Road [to the right] and Thurstaston Road [to the left]* **Irby,** *dated back to c.1640. This Elizabethan farm house was described by Beazley as a "little gem" being a small stone house with mullioned and hooded windows [see 1960]*[T]

Right: *Mr RA King's Farman Biplane is seen on the shore at* **Parkgate** *on 16 July 1912. He flew from Freshfield, near Liverpool, along the Wirral coast over* **New Brighton, Hoylake** *and* **Heswall** *landing on the shore at Parkgate at 8.30pm. This was recorded as the first visit of an aeroplane to Parkgate [see 1914]*

Left: *Looking along Thingwall Road towards* **Irby** *village when it was a country lane. The castelated building on the right was known as* Vine Cottage *and was lived in about this time by a Miss Bithell and by 1923 Thomas Louis West. The house is still there today with an altered frontage and now called* Minook *[see 1909]*

1913

- Miss May Richardson opened a girls' school in *Moorside Cottage*, Moorside Lane **Neston** [see 1918]N
- St Michael's Mission Church built in **Little Neston**N
- Talbot Estate **Little Neston** sold including: *White House Farm* [113 acres]; *Ivy Farm* [93 acres]; *Rock Farm* [73 acres]; *Rose Farm* [66 acres]; *Mellock Farm* [10 acres]; + two smaller farms - *Ashtree Farm* and *Lees Lane Farm*N

Feb   The schooner *Guiding Star* was stranded at **Thurstaston** shore [see photo next page]

Above: *Burton* Manor had been enlarged and remodelled in 1904 by Sir Charles Nicholson for Henry Neville Gladstone including a small inner courtyard - he also designed **Burton** vicarage [see 1912 and 1958]

Right: *The only house in Pipers Lane* **Heswall** *looking towards Thurstaston is the newly-built* Sven Tor *- when the lane was no more than a dirt track with no foundations [see below]*

Right: *Looking from the opposite direction to the picture above towards Delavor Road shows* Sven Tor *the only house in Pipers Lane* **Heswall**

Below: *This is a close-up of* Sven Tor *which is seen in the two photographs above right. This turreted building still stands overlooking Pipers Lane* **Heswall** *today*

Above: *The St Mary and St Helen's Church Vicarage, which is pictured in Parkgate Road* **Neston***, was erected c.1906C. It is also seen in the background of the 1908 photograph of the 4th Lancashire RFA*

Above: *According to the two postcards of the picnicers posing for the photograph at* **Irby** Hill Farm *and in front of the chapel [below] they were on a church ramble*
Below: *The picnicers seen above are now posing in front of the Methodist Chapel Mill Hill Road* **Irby** *[see 1919 and 1930]*

Below: *The Congregationalists erected this wooden chapel in* **Neston in** *1909 with 400 sittings but due to lack of support closed in 1927, reopened in 1929 but finally closed in 1938 - it is now the site of the British Legion*

Above: *This vessel, the* Guiding Star, *is pictured stranded at* **Thurstaston** *on 18 February 1913*

Above: *The* **Bidston** *to* **Hawarden** *Bridge railway line opened for goods 16 March 1896 and passengers 18 May 1896. The* **Burton** *Point Railway Station pictured here was opened on 1 August 1899. This station was never very busy and closed 1955[PWR]*

Right: *Looking down High Street* **Neston** *just before the First World War. This shows how narrow the High Street was beyond this point - but it was 50 years before all the buildings on the right had been demolished and the road widened [see 1959]. Within a year many of the men pictured, together with others from the village, would exchange this peaceful scene for the battlefields of France*

– Centenary of **Neston** Female Friendly Society [see photo][N]

– **Parkgate** Convalescent Home and **Neston** Institute taken over as Red Cross hospitals[N]

Jul 4 A local branch of the The Camping Club of Great Britain - named the Lancashire, Cheshire and North Wales District Association, which had been established on 23 June, held their first official camp at **Heswall**[TWM]

Jul 8 Henri Salmet arrived at **Parkgate** with his Bleirot 80hp seven-cylinder Gnome Monoplane on a lorry - he was based at Parks Field and for three days gave short trips to the paying public [see photos next page][N]

Aug 22 Mrs R Tidswell offered *Bank House* **Heswall** [see next page] as a soldiers' convalescent hospital [VS]

Sep 3 Recruiting meeting at **Heswall** presided over by Mr Charles MacIver JP CC[BNVS]

Oct 6 Belgian refugees arrive at *Tower House* **Heswall**[VS]

*Above: This was part of the procession for the **Neston Female Friendly Society** - which was very special that year as they celebrated their centenary. The society was founded in 1814 with members subscribing regularly to its fund and could claim financial assistance in times of illness, childbirth or death. The society is still in existence today and celebrates on the first Thursday of June each year - it is the only one of its type to survive today[YWPH]*

*Right: **Heswall** Church Lads' Brigade Band are posing for a photograph*

*Above: This was Mackie and Gladstone's Rock Wine and Spirit Stores in Dee View Road **Heswall** just before the lease expired in 1914. The site is now the car park for the Dee View Hotel*

*Above: The flags are flying on The Parade at **Parkgate** with most people watching the regatta - except for the boy on the bench who is fast asleep! The Parkgate Regatta dated back to 1827. The last of the traditional Parkgate Fishermen's Regatta was held 11 July 1914 with races for both sail [see photo] and oars; nobbies, yawls and punts; rowing and sculling; races for fishermen etc*

*Above: Leighton Garage - operated by EG Davis, Automotive Engineer, was situated on the Chester High Road at **Leighton** opposite Boathouse Lane. Part of this site became a garage with showroom[YW6]*

1914 continued

Above: *Henri Salmet, the French aviator, is seen in **Parkgate** with an admirer - he was in Parkgate for three days. Salmet was the chief flight instructor at the Bleriot Flight School Hendon and made a nonstop flight of 222 miles from London to Paris in 2 hours 57 minutes in a Bleriot monoplane 7 March 1912. The Cheshire Automobile Club arranged for Salmet, who was on a publicity tour with the* Daily Mail, *to give an aviation display at Park Fields **Parkgate** [see photos]*

Above: *Members of the Cheshire Automobile Club, organisers of the event, are inspecting the 80 hp Bleriot-Gnome monoplane which is on Park Fields **Parkgate** 8 July 1914 with the aviator Henri Salmet. Looking closely at the aeroplane the words* Daily *and* Mail *can be seen on the underside of the aeroplane wings with the tyres looking no bigger than those on a bicycle!*

Below: *The 80 hp Bleriot-Gnome monoplane with Henri Salmet at the controls is airborne over Park Fields **Parkgate**. The tent on the left housed the aeroplane and the white marquee on the right was for corporate entertainment - the middle one is a haystack [seen above]*

Above: *These mainly young men of **Heswall** had gathered for a group photograph in civilian uniform, in The Mount with Pensby Road behind, before signing up as volunteers in September - mainly for the Cheshire Regiment. By Christmas 1914, most of them were fighting in France - some of them never returned [see 1924]*

1915

- The Wirral Colliery (1915) Ltd took over running of **Little Neston** Colliery[N]
- The **Neston** Picturedrome Company, which had shown films in the Neston Institute, moved to the Town Hall because the Institute had become a military hospital[YW6]
- The military opened a recruiting Office at **Neston** Town Hall[N]

Jan 18   Soldier's Club opened at **Heswall**[VS]

Above: *The Royal Liverpool Children's Hospital Telegraph Road **Heswall** was built on a nine acre site which was purchased for £2,500 in 1900. The foundation stone was laid 21 April 1905 and following fundraising events, the first patients were admitted February 1909. It was deemed at the time that fresh air was the answer to most ailments - hence the children had been wheeled out of the hospital on their beds. The open-air balcony above led onto the wards and the children's beds would be put out each night throughout the year, regardless of weather*

Above: *St Michael's Church **Shotwick** is seen from across the fields. When Shotwick was the main port for **Chester**, before the River Dee silted up and ships became larger, boats once moored near the wall surrounding the church*

Below: *This play on words was a popular theme for comic postcards of this era - as seen on this postcard sent from **Neston***

Above: *Taken from the 'Donkey Stand' the horse and carriage on the left on the Parade **Parkgate** must have belonged to one of the local dignitaries as the coach-man has a top hat. Mostyn House School is seen in the background and a landing stage for small boats is seen on the right*

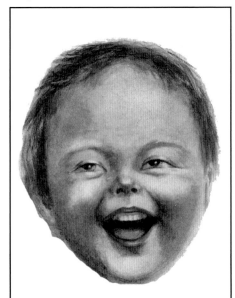

A little Sun and 'Air from NESTON.

Left: *Looking down Riverbank Road **Lower Heswall** towards the River Dee and Welsh Hills beyond. The houses on the right date back to 1896 and are still there today. This was the main road from Heswall Railway Station for the the many people who travelled by train for a day out on Heswall beach*

JOHN R. GOODALL,
MONUMENTAL SCULPTOR,
Mersey View, Telegraph Road,
HESWALL.

—o—

Monumental Work in Granite, Marble and Stone.
Inscriptions Cut Accurately.
Renovations, &c.
Designs and Estimates on Application

Above: *The extension to the left of **Heswall** Castle was to accommodate more girls for the orphanage [see 1906]. The castle was demolished c.1935 and Castle buildings Telegraph Road **Heswall** erected near the site in 1936*

Above: *A group of fishermen are congregating in the centre of The Parade at the south end of **Parkgate** whilst to the left and right of them are businessmen hurrying along*

Above: *The caption on this postcard read: "**Neston** and District Ambulance Brigade **Parkgate** Convalescent Home 19 September 1914". There were men of all ages photographed by their stretchers - they were responsible for collecting some of the wounded soldiers returning from France via **Birkenhead** Woodside station and then looking after them at the convalescent home*

Below: ***Neston** Institute in Hinderton Road became a Red Cross Hospital from 1914 to 1918, treating wounded soldiers sent home from the battlefront. The building is now known as the Civic Hall [see 1904]*

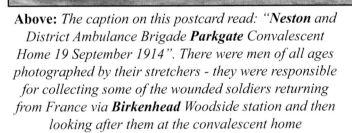

Having a Pick-Me-Up at
HESWALL

Above: *This was a typical comic postcard of the time - sent from **Heswall***

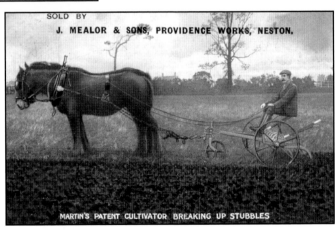

SOLD BY
J. MEALOR & SONS, PROVIDENCE WORKS, NESTON.

MARTIN'S PATENT CULTIVATOR BREAKING UP STUBBLES

Above: *This advertising postcard was for 'J Mealor & Sons, Providence Works **Neston**'- although based in Burton Road **Ness** they probably used the name Neston as that was the nearest railway station. The business was started c.1851 by Samuel and Margaret Mealor although 1880 is the company's foundation date. Over the decades the firm invented and developed agricultural instruments, manufactured railings and shod horses from their forge [see 1903]. They are still in business there today*

NESTON INSTITUTE

1916

- Johnny Pye operated a bus service from Kings Hall Telegraph Road **Heswall** to a munitions factory at **Queensferry** [see 1921][N]

Jan 27 Wirral Farmers' Sale realised £100 for **Neston** Red Cross Hospital[VS]

Feb 3 New **Neston** Auxiliary Hospital opened for inspection[VS]

Mar 13 Mr AV Paton presented over 27 acres of land at **Thurstaston** as a memorial to the Wirral men who gave their lives in the great war[VS]

Jul 20 Major William La Touche Congreve was awarded a posthumous VC for his brave action at Longueval on the Somme [see text 1899][NEWS]

Above: *These were the outbuildings for the munitions factory set up by Mr Whinneray during the First World War in the grounds of his house* Leighton Court *Buggen Lane* **Neston** *[see below]*

Above: *The old gentleman is photographed from Gayton Lane* **Gayton** *with the toll bar behind him in Chester High Road. Gayton Toll Bar was a collection point for travellers on the* **Chester** *to* **Heswall** *road and beyond. This delightful four-roomed cottage was last lived in 1965 then sold in 1979 for £15,000. However, plans to renovate and extend the cottage were turned down in 1981. All that remains today is a square sandstone windowless building*[YW6]

Above: *Mr Whinneray [see photo above] on the left working with one of his assistants*

Above: *This was an advertising postcard for Hadfield's Special Turnip Manure with Mr Clement Bower of* Little Gayton Farm *who successfully grew their manure - the gentleman in the cart with a top hat was Hadfield's agent*

Left: *Burton Rocks were once lofty sandstone cliffs, since worn and rounded by the River Dee and then the face cut away to provide material for an embankment. In 1877, 29 skeletons were discovered near here with the conclusion that they were probably the crew of a vessel wrecked on the rocks*[THW]

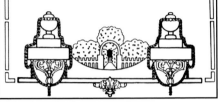

Above: *The* Plough Inn *is pictured at the far end of the row of cottages in Park Street* **Neston** *at its junction with Cross Street. The inn closed about this time during the First World War [see page 1881]*

Above: Heswall *Parish Church of St Peter is seen in lower village looking across the graveyard in the opposite direction to the 1899 photograph [see page 27]*

Above: *Bishop Wilson's thatched cottage stood in The Village* **Burton**. *He was born here in 1663 and for 58 years was Bishop of Sodor and Man. When he died he was buried in an elm coffin which had come from a tree he planted when a young man*

Left: *This was a postcard sent by a sweetheart who is depicted sitting at home in* **Neston** *thinking of her loved one whilst writing a letter to him. He is pictured in a thought bubble in the trenches*

Above: Yew Tree Farm *is pictured on the right in Thingwall Road* **Irby**. *Standing opposite the* Prince of Wales Inn *[see 1899], parts of the building dated back to the 17th late century. In November 1919 the farm had 86 acres of pasture and arable land with a nursery of 20,000 fruit trees. After being derelict for some years, it was taken over in 1980 by the Yew Tree Community Trust - an organisation sponsored by the Methodist Churches of* **Moreton** *and* **Irby** *to train 16 to 18 year olds*

1917

- The former home of the Ismay family *Dawpool* **Thurstaston** was handed over for use as an orthopaedic hospital for officers by the then owner Mr FWP Rutter - it opened in 1918
- **Heswall** Operatic Society was formed - their first performance was *Martha*
- St Thomas' Church **Parkgate** purchased by the Church of England - formerly a non-conformist chapel[N]

Oct 21 Mr HN Gladstone presented badges to **Neston** VAD men at **Parkgate** military hospital[VS]

Nov 3 Matron at **Parkgate** Hospital received Royal Red Cross Distinction[VS]

Above: *This rear view of the Glegg Arms **Gayton** was taken from the bowling green [see 1896]. A beer garden and children's play area now occupy the site*

Above: *These children from Charles Thompson's Mission, were collected from **Ledsham** Station in this wonderful car and transported to Puddington Hall for a day out*

HENRY SWIFT,
COAL MERCHANT,

Depot HESWALL STATION.

Best Lancashire, North Wales, and Neston Coals, delivered in Carts, or supplied per Waggon Load at Heswall Station.

ALL ORDERS BY POST PROMPTLY ATTENDED TO.
Private Address   THE NEST, HESWALL.

Right: *The building on the left, described as the Old Ferry House **Gayton**, was marked on Greenwood's 1819 map of Cheshire as operating a ferry service to Flintshire. It was recorded in 1277 that Edward I crossed from Gayton to Flint after a stay at **Shotwick** Castle. It stands today at the bottom of Cottage Lane Gayton [see 1910]*

Above: *These were the steps leading down to the beach at the south end of **Parkgate** - Mostyn House School is the tall building with a flag pole in the background, pictured on The Parade. The message on the back of the postcard, which was sent in August 1915, said "We've 2,000 soldiers here camping in the field [Park Fields] by the Station*

Above: *This view was taken from the top of **Neston** Mill looking along Leighton Road towards Neston town centre. The mill was built of tower construction in the mid 18th century and ceased operating in the 1880s. It lay derelict for decades until 1975 when it had a new lease of life as The Old Mill Gallery which was a glass engraving business, ceasing in 1990 when Bob Ellison retired [see 1911]*

Above: *This comic postcard shows a child - who has been given a penny - heading to buy an ice cream so the young couple can have a quick embrace while he is away. It was sent from **Heswall** in 1917*

Above: *Looking along the shore line at **Thurstaston**. the cottage in the distance was known as* Coastguard's *or later* Sally's Cottage. *The wooden structure on the right was steps onto the beach*

Above: *This arch once stood on **Thurstaston** shore. Beazley in his book* Thurstaston *said: "A tiny stream flows into the Dee. On the shore at this point is a massive archway of the local red sandstone, some of the stones being as much as 6ft. long. From this point a jetty runs into the sea while the beach is strewn with squared stones. At some point there had been a quay or sea wall to protect the bank against erosion and the archway was made to allow the stream access to the sea." This could be part of the wall mentioned with the stream not apparent and the archway in a ruinous state [see 1928]. The little dale seen through the arch was filled in by the Wirral Urban District Council*[WBB]

Left: *This was a close-up photograph of the Parkgate Convalescent Home on The Parade at **Parkgate**. During the First World War it was used as a Red Cross Hospital where some of the locals are photographed with the wounded soldiers [see 1915]. The building had an unusual square facade, which was built to shore up the front of the building. It was demolished in the 1950s*

- EC Whineray of *Leighton Court* **Neston** donated a motor ambulance to Neston Council[N]
- Shop, smithy, 3 cottages and land **Irby** sold at auction £1,375[LCPSR]
- Miss May Richardson moved her girls' school from Moorside Lane [see 1907] to a house called *Leighton* [later to become the ***Parkgate Hotel***]. It closed in 1939 and the premises were taken over by the army [see photo][N]
- The two semi-detached houses on the front at **Parkgate** built in 1863 were bought by AG Grenfell, Headmaster of Mostyn House School, and converted into *Holywell House*, then initially used as a boarding house for 40 boarders and in 1923 became *Holywell Temperance Hotel*

Apr 17 *Dawpool* at **Thurstaston** opened as a military hospital [see 1917][VS]

Oct 12 Frank Lester from **Irby** was killed in action and was later awarded a posthumous VC for his action[YW6]

Above: *Christ Church Barnston Vicarage, built of local sandstone, is pictured in Barnston Road* **Barnston***. It was first used 31 July 1880 [see 1936]*[SOUV]

Above: *This is where the railway track for the Wirral Colliery ended. This branch line was added to the* **Parkgate** *to* **Hooton** *line, which had opened in 1866, following the sinking of a new shaft in 1874. The second locomotive employed to haul the coal trucks to the sidings at* **Neston** *was the* Lord Talbot *which had been built in 1881. By 1926 [a year before the colliery closed], there were an estimated 10 coal wagons a day - in the earlier years the number was much greater[see 1906]*[N]

Above: *The distinctive black and white half-timbered buildings belonged to Mostyn House School* **Parkgate***. The tall building on the extreme right was a well disguised water tower*

Above: *This was the entrance to Miss May Richardson's Leighton Day and Boarding School for Girls* **Parkgate** *which she had opened here c.1918. The building had been erected in 1862 for Joseph Rich, who had moved from High Street* **Neston***, and had called it* Rich Villa***.** *However, he was declared bankrupt within three years! By c.1900 it was called* Leighton *and after Miss Richardson retired and closed the school in 1938, it was taken over by the military in 1940. After the war it became the* Leighton Hotel *and then* Parkgate Hotel*. The building is still there today as a private property with new properties built in the grounds*

Above: *The* Old Quay House **Ness** *was first mentioned in 1640 - being an inn until c.1710 when it became three dwellings. In 1750 it was leased to the County of Cheshire, being used as the Neston House of Correction where Irish vagrants were housed before being deported to Dublin. After 1803 it became a private house until c.1915. Having been derelict for years it was blown up as part of a Home Guard exercise in the early 1940s*

1918 continued

Left: *This unusual photograph shows the foundations for the Crosshill Reservoir* **Thingwall** *in the process of being constructed. During the building of the reservoir, the licensee of the* Prince of Wales Inn *Thingwall Road* **Irby** *supplied the workmen with beer and stout which he sold illegally from a cart - a pint of beer cost 2.5d but he was fined £10! On 9/10 January 1941 a string of bombs, which were probably aimed at the Thingwall Reservoir caused damage to Nos.2 to 12 Berwyn Avenue and 70 to 88 Pensby Road. One of the bombs fell in Barnston Road near Dale End Road, which seriously damaged the water main, with Holmwood Avenue and* Top House Farm *also affected[BW]*

Right: Elder Cottage *is the larger thatched sandstone cottage on the left in Thurstaston Road* **Lower Heswall**. *Dating back to 1686, it was the original school - in 1847 there were 60 pupils. In 1872 the school moved to new purpose-built premises in School Hill.* Elder Cottage *was demolished in 1954 and the road widened. The* Heswall Hotel *is seen on the extreme right [see 1940]. The smaller building on the left dated from 1840 and t the time of this picture it was the library*

Above: *Boys from Mostyn House School* **Parkgate** *are land sailing on the sands of the River Dee - this was an ideal site for land yachts when the tide was out with plenty of sand and strong winds. Today there is not even a grain of sand to be seen here*

Right: *The half-timbered* Sunnybank Cottage *is seen on a sandstone outcrop on the right in The Village* **Burton** *[see 1904]*

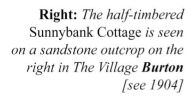

1919

- John Pye started operating a bus service between **Heswall** and **Birkenhead** using Kings Hall Heswall as his depot [see 1921][TWCB]
- **Shotwick** War Memorial unveiled at St Michael's Church
- Lever Brothers acquired land at **Thurstaston** where a camp was created for their employees [see 1932][YW6]
- Our Lady and St John Catholic Church opened a temporary church in Telegraph Road **Heswall**[HDS]

Above: *Pickerton Cottage, which is seen on the right in Neston Road* **Burton**, *dates back to at least 1810 when it was a pub called the* Earth Stopper *rented by Edward and Ann Medlicott - by 1822 the victualler was John Cooper. There was a hole in the wall, seen between the door and window, which was said to have been used to either pass jugs of ale through during unlicensed hours or to sailors not welcome inside but would supply them through the hole - taking their money first!* Stanley House *was the half-timbered cottage to the left, which was once the* Stanley Arms *[see 1905]*

Above: *Shotwick Village is seen from St Michael's Church tower which shows the cluster of cottages forming the centre of this small village. The cottage with the dark side in the centre was once the* Greyhound Inn *which held illegal weddings in the 17th century [see 1887]*

Above: *The horse and cart on the left standing outside the shop and Post Office in* **Irby** *which belonged to Edward Jones - the publisher of this postcard. He later became the Postmaster here with his daughter running the Post Office, as he also had a shop in* **Greasby** *village. The* Prince of Wales *pub is in the background [see 1899]*

Above: *Sid Reddy, son of Charles Reddy who owned a butcher's shop in Pensby Road* **Heswall**, *had his own butcher's shop here in The Lydiate* **Lower Heswall**. *Later the property became 'Shocky' Shone's paint shop and today is* Annabel's Cottage

Above Right: *The caption on this postcard read "**Thurstaston** Encampment". The site was at the bottom of Station Road* **Thurstaston**. *The caravans were pulled there by horse with the owners of the tents beyond travelling by train to the nearby Thurstaston Station. This area is still popular today, but with more substantial holiday homes overlooking the River Dee*

Above: *The tin chapel which belonged to the Primitive Methodists, is seen on the right in the stack yard of* Irby Hill Farm ***Irby*** *[see 1887]. It was on land to the right of the chapel that the first ever official scout camp was held in 1908, following the inauguration of the Scout Movement in* **Birkenhead** *YMCA by Baden Powell. In the 1950s an American gentleman contacted the local Scout leader Mr Duddleston and together they visited Dodd's* Irby Hill Farm. *The American was shown the site of the first camp and standing on the spot he solemnly stated: "From that camp fire has the light been carried to light all camp fires of the world". He wanted to erect a memorial on the site, but Ethel Dodd dissuaded him*[YW6]

Above: *The* Rookery Farm *farmhouse is pictured in Thingwall Road* **Irby**. *Mr Arthur Constantine had purchased the farm in 1916 with a tenant farmer Mr Jones staying on until the early 1920s. The land was sold and the farmhouse was used by the Irby Literary Society who met here. In the early 1930s, following an idea suggested by Frank Dodd and Joe Roberts, the vacant building became the Irby and District Social Club, which opened to members in 1933. The farm outbuildings were demolished and Irby Mission, together with the block of shops on the corner of Mill Hill Road, was built on the site. Teddy Kendrick was the boy driving the donkey milk cart and the girl became Connie Andrews. The building is still there today, now known as the Irby Club*

1920

Mar 25 *Thingwall* Hall gifted in Miss MC Twigge's will as a country home for sick children - occupied by The Royal Liverpool Children's Hospital [see photo this page][YWPH]

Jun Neston War Memorial Cottage Hospital opened in **Little Neston** with 21 beds [see photo][N]

Aug 29 Neston War Memorial erected in St Mary's churchyard **Neston** with 91 names of those local men who died[N]

*Above: This large sandstone house just off The Green in **Little Neston** called* Dee View *had belonged to William Pritchard. However, when the Red Cross Hospital in **Neston** Institute closed at the end of the First World War [see 1915] it was decided to use the funds remaining towards buying* Dee View. *The 'Neston War Memorial Cottage Hospital' was opened June 1920 by Lord Leverhulme - initially it had 21 beds[N]*

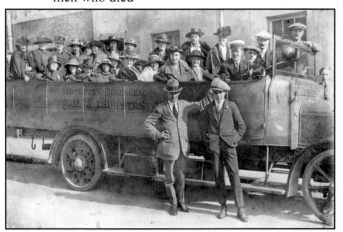

Above: *The sign on the charabanc with solid tyres said: 'JG Richardson Elmswood Road **Birkenhead** - **Heswall** and **Thurstaston'**. John Richardson who had a charabanc business from c.1920 until the early 1930s, applied for a licence for the **Irby** to Birkenhead route, but was unsuccessful as John Pye already used the route. However, not one to give up, he approached Arthur Constantine who owned* Rookery Farm **Irby** *and obtained permission to pick up passengers from his farmyard [it was legal then to operate on private land]*

Above: *This was the front view of* Thingwall Hall *which was erected in 1849 for Captain Lilley, a merchant in the African Trade. By the turn of the 20th century, Mr Edward Twigge was the owner and also the first Captain of **Heswall** Golf Club. Mr Twigge's daughter, Muriel, gave the hall to the Royal Liverpool Children's Hospital c.1920. In 1960 the hall was demolished and flats erected on the site in 1962. The gate posts still stand either side of the entrance to Torrington Drive at Thingwall Corner*

Above: *This snow scene was taken in Gayton Lane **Gayton** before the road became developed*

Above right: *Looking across Oldfield Road **Heswall** [from bottom left to centre right] towards the River Dee and North Wales beyond. The buildings in the centre formed Cleaver Sanitorium which was named after Mr HP Cleaver who was the inspiration behind its founding, opening in 1902. It became a children's hospital by 1913 but after the children were evacuated to **Rhuddlan** in 1939 adult patients moved in. From 1950 it changed its name to Cleaver Hospital and the hospital closed down with the land being sold in 1988 for £2.5 million [see 1907]*

1920 continued

Above: *Neston Comrades Amateur Football Club photographed in the 1919/20 season*

Above: *Sergeant Bee is pictured in front of Neston Cross. A well known character in the area, he married Emily Boumphrey from Heswall [see school photo 1882]. Family legend has it that when they came out of the church after the service at St Peter's Church Lower Heswall, a 'hurdy girdy' man played the tune 'You are the Honeysuckle, I am the Bee' on a barrel organ with a monkey on top!*

Above: *This was the front entrance to* **Thurstaston** *Hall. The hall can be traced back to 1070 when Hugh Lupus presented the manor and other estates in Wirral and North Wales to his relative Robert de Rodelent. There is a possibility that a building existed then on the present site of the hall. The oldest portion standing is the west wing dating back to c.1350. In 1680 the central portion was built with a curious roof-wall bearing the crest of the Glegg family. The east wing was added in 1835. An unusual fact is that the hall, which is said to be haunted, has never been for sale as it has been passed from generation to generation [see 1933]*

Right: The Bull and Dog Inn *Little Neston, which was very popular with the miners from the local colliery, dated back to at least 1822 when John Sutton was the victualler. In the 1850 and 1860 directories, when WilliamRoberts was the victualler, it was referred to as* The Bull *and again in 1896 it was* The Bull *with Matthew Roberts the landlord [probably a relative of William Roberts]. The* **Birkenhead** *Brewery dray No.24 is seen outside the inn and the name on the side of the building confirms it was then* The Bull & Dog Inn. *By 1923 it had been converted into two private houses*

65

1921

- The erection of the **Thingwall** Sanitorium commenced for the County Borough of **Birkenhead** [see 1929][KD]
- Lever Brothers Holiday Camp opened at **Thurstaston** for the use of their employees [see 1932][YWPH]

Mar — All coal mines passed out of Government control - **Neston** miners went on strike - ended July when miners were forced to accept a pay reduction[N]

Apr 18 — The *New Cinema* opened in **Neston** - seated 508[TSSW]

Jul — The **Parkgate** Regatta, which was first organised in 1827, was held for the last time[N]

Above: *This picturesque snow scene was taken in* **Barnston** *Dale*

Above: *This quarry which was off Thursaston Road was one of several sandstone quarries in* **Heswall** *from which many of the local houses and cottages were built*

Left: *Three of John Pye's motor vehicles are seen outside his bus station in Telegraph Road* **Heswall**. *The building was opened in 1912 as the* King's Hall *with John Pye operating from here in 1916 when he ran a bus service from Heswall to a munitions factory in* **Queensferry**. *After the First World War he started operating a service from* **Heswall** *to* **Birkenhead** *[see photo] and by the time he sold the business to Crosville in 1924 he had a fleet of 21 buses. John Pye also operated a cinema here from 1916 and modernised it in 1928 when it could seat 900. He sold out in the mid 1930s [see 1950]*

Right: *This was John Pye's Heswall and Birkenhead Motor Bus Co timetable and fares from September 1922 until further notice. This gives details of the* **Heswall, Thurstaston** *and* **Birkenhead** *[Singleton Avenue] route and also the* **Parkgate, Neston** *and Birkenhead [Singleton Avenue] route. John Pye was not allowed to be in competition with the Birkenhead Corporation transport so was only allowed to travel as far as the bottom of Singleton Avenue, where he built a bus station. He also advertised motor charabancs, touring cars and taxis for hire [see right]*[WB]

HESWALL AND BIRKENHEAD MOTOR BUS CO.

PROPRIETOR J. PYE.

TIME-TABLE and FARES. on and after September 1st, and until further notice.

HESWALL, THURSTASTON & BIRKENHEAD (Singleton Avenue).

SPECIAL CHAR-A-BANCS direct for Irby and Thurstaston Shore. Leave Singleton Avenue week-days 10-0 a.m. and 2-0 p.m., returning 7-0 and 8-30 p.m. Sundays at 10-30 a.m., 1-0 p.m., and hourly till 8-0 p.m. Fare, Single 1/3. Return, 2/-.

PARKGATE, NESTON AND BIRKENHEAD.

MOTOR CHAR-A-BANCS & TOURING CARS FOR HIRE.

TAXIS FOR HIRE.

PHONE—HESWALL 108.

1922

–   Neston Cricket Club purchased their ground at **Parkgate**[FYNC]

June   **Heswall** Golf Club course returned to 18 holes - there had been 18 holes from at least 1906 but during the First World War some of the holes had been ploughed up for the war effort. An exhibition match was played to celebrate the occasion[HGC]

Above: Stacey's is the near two thirds of the thatched cottage seen in Village Road **Lower Heswall.** *It stood opposite to* Roscote, *the country home of Thomas Brocklebank the shipping magnate [see 1928]. To the left of the car was a general stores with a smithy behind [see 1911] and the building behind the man in the distance was Pennington's shop*

Above: *This imposing building was* Gayton Hall *Gayton. It was described by Sulley in 1889: "Gayton Hall, 'till lately the residence of the Glegg Family, is a fine well situated mansion, commanding the estuary of the Dee, and standing in well-wooded grounds. During the period when* **Parkgate** *and* **Dawpool** *were the chief ports of embarkation for Ireland, it was famous for the hospitality extended to travellers, and was honoured in 1689 by a visit from William III, when on his way to Ireland. His Majesty conferred the honour of knighthood in return on its then owner, William Glegg"*

Right: *The* Wheatsheaf Inn *at Ness, which was originally in Well Lane but moved here in 1842, was mentioned in a directory of 1850 when the victualler was Joseph Cabry. The inn was sold at auction in October 1893 for £2,100. In 1896 the licensee was John Green who was still here in 1923 about the time this photo was taken. At one time the inn was extended to the right with darker brick used [see 1959]*

Left: *Looking along Telegraph Road* **Heswall** *towards the junction with Pensby Road on the right and The Mount on the left, just beyond the cars. Behind the fence on right was land which belonged to John Pye who operated the motor bus service and cinema from the former* Kings Hall *seen just beyond the canopy on the right [see previous page]. When Crosville took over John Pye's motor bus company in 1924, the land came with the deal. It was here that they built the Heswall Bus depot. Heswall Fire Station was built on land to the left opening in 1940*

1923

- **Parkgate** Convalescent Home on The Parade was purchased - renamed *Rigby House* and used as a holiday home in summer and for local charities in winter [see 1917][N]
- Old Caldians Rugby Club founded[CGGS]
- Apr Originally The Slack and then Slack Road **Heswall** - it changed its name to Milner Road [see photo of *Sandon Arms* 1925][NEWS]
- May 12 **Parkgate** open-air baths opened - built for Mr AG Grenfell, Headmaster of Mostyn House School - initially for school use only but later opened it up to the public [see photo 1932][N]

Above: *The caption on this advertising postcard for "Lieut. Mike Rimmington's Reformatory and Riding School, Station Road **Parkgate** by **Chester**" was 'Mankillers Converted'*

Right: *The lady on the left is posting a letter outside **Irby** Post Office Thingwall Road with the name HC Leech above the door*

Above: *This was an advert for J Roberts' Hillside Farm **Thurstaston** [see below]*

Above: *This was a weekend holiday home facing the shore called Westward Ho in an area known as The Looms at the bottom of Banks Road **Heswall**, in the lane opposite the car park. The Council tried to have them demolished in 1939 but the Ministry of Health decided they were suitable for holiday purposes*

Left: *These were the girls and boys of Charles Thompson Mission **Birkenhead**, with their helpers, on a picnic. The tables were set for tea time at Robert's Hillside Farm in School Lane **Thurstaston** which was popular for outings because of its proximity to Thurstaston Hill. It was also a good venue due to the corrugated iron building behind which would could be used if the weather was bad [see advert above and 1934]*

1924

– The *Old Mill Cafe* and Stores Mill Lane **Irby** opened by George and Bertha Lumsden - known locally as *Lumsden's Cafe* [see 1938][YWPH]

– **Heswall** Gospel Hall opened in Pensby Road[SOUV]

Jan 20 **Heswall** Golf Club clubhouse, which was built entirely of pitch pine, was burnt down - estimated damage £10,000[YW6]

Jan 22 Crosville took over Johnny Pye's bus company for £25,000 including £7,500 in shares - he retained the *Kings Hall* from which he operated the *King's Cinema* [see 1921][TWCB]

Apr 13 **Heswall** War Memorial unveiled [see photos]

Above: *The **Heswall** War Memorial is being unveiled on 13 April 1924 in memory of the men of Heswall and District who were killed in the First World War*

Above: *Scouts and Guides were among the procession walking with the crowd down Dee View **Heswall** towards the War Memorial for the unveiling ceremony [see photo right and above right]*

Right: *This was a close-up view of the **Heswall** War Memorial seen above*

Below: *This was a comic postcard from **Heswall***

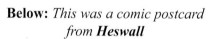

Above: *This old cottage once stood in Gayton Road **Lower Heswall** with Station Road off to the right. It is said that a 'Tiger' Smith once lived here. This thatched cottage and the stone one beyond were both demolished in the 1930s and the site is now a grassed area [see 1937][YW1]*

1925

— Approval given to **Neston** UDC to build eight houses in Raby Road [*Raby Gardens*] and 16 houses at **Parkgate** [*Mostyn Gardens*][N]

Jul **Heswall** Golf Club's new clubhouse was completed - the old one having been destroyed by fire in 1924[HGC]

Nov 14 Foundation stone for the Parish Church Hall was laid on land behind the Church of the Good Shepherd **Heswall**[SOUV]

Left: *This was a photograph of the **Irby** Supper Bar in Mill Hill Road which was featured in the Wirral Society's cautionary guide due to the litter!*

Left: Dale House Farm *Storeton Lane* **Barnston** *was a very popular venue for picnics, special treats and Sunday school outings. It operated from c.1900 to just before the Second World War. Initially it offered a tearoom and picnic area [indoors if wet]. There were 15 acres of grounds for children to explore and later on there were swings, a small indoor roundabout for the younger children, a large 'chair-o-plane' for the older children [as seen in the photo] and a long wooden slide [see 1931]*[BPV]

Right: *There were two beerhouses in The Slack* **Heswall** *from at least 1874 - the* Sandon Arms *and* Ebenezer Arms. *The road name changed in April 1925 to Milner Road where the* Sandon Arms *is seen with 'hotel' on the chimney. George Smith, a former stonemason, is pictured on the left in front of his cottage where they raised at least seven children. The cottages were bought by the brewery and demolished in 1981 - the site is now the pub car park*

Left: *This aerial view of* **Parkgate** *shows the south end of The Parade. The cluster of houses to the right of the very white house, which faced onto Station Road, were all demolished in the early 1960s to make way for the Birkenhead Brewery Old Quay pub [see 1960]. The tall tower centre left was the Mostyn House School water tower [see 1906] with the main school buildings on the extreme left. The* **Hooton** *to* **West Kirby** *railway line is seen travelling across fields in a slight curve from near the top right edge*

1926

- A safe robbery at **Heswall** Station was interrupted by Police Constable Mullins who tried to arrest the three men [see next page]
- The coal miners families from **Neston** did not go hungry during the General Strike due to the generosity of Mrs Bulley [wife of Arthur Bulley, founder of Ness Gardens][N]
- **Heswall** Parish Hall erected at a cost of £4,600[KD]
- *Boathouse Cafe* **Parkgate** opened on the site of the *Pengwern Arms*[N]
- The third **Neston** Telephone Exchange opened in Leighton Road [it closed in 1968 being replaced with a purpose built one]

Jun   New **Heswall** Golf Club clubhouse opened - replaced the wooden clubhouse burnt down [see 1924][HGC]

Jun 17   An RAF bi-plane crash-landed onto **Heswall** Golf Club course - Pilot Officer Pentland's life was saved by using a parachute [see photo next page][HGC]

Sep 18   Garden party in aid of the **Hoylake** and **West Kirby** Cottage Hospital held at *Dawpool* **Thurstaston** - this was the last function held at the former residence of the Ismay family before it was demolished[YW6]

Above: *The front of the Akbar Nautical School is seen in Green Lane off Oldfield Drive* **Heswall**. *The* Akbar *was originally a training ship moored in the River Mersey off* **New Ferry**. *They moved here to a shore base in 1907 when the new buildings cost over £17,000. The only part of the building remaining today is that on the far right behind the flag pole. The school closed down in 1956 and the site sold with private homes built there*[YW6]

Right: *This comic postcard, which shows a young maid waking an excited old man up with his breakfast, was posted in* **Heswall**

Above: *Elm Stores is seen on the left, the proprietor being B Clarke, in Thingwall Road* **Irby** *[see 1933]. The whitewashed cottages beyond are still there today and the scouts, who were probably camping in the area, are standing outside the single-storied Post Office. The former* Prince of Wales Inn *is pictured in the background - it ceased being a pub by 1923 [see 1899]*[YW6]

Right: *Jean Smallwood is standing on the steps outside her bakery and general stores in* **Lower Heswall**. *The single-storied building just to the left was the purpose-built Post Office, opening in 1899. Originally the Post Office was in the Smallwood's bakery shop but the authorities would not allow the Post Office to operate in the same building. Shops now occupy the site beyond the Post Office with* Elder Cottage *seen in the background*[YW6]

1926 continued

Above: *Pilot Officer Pentland's RAF bi-plane crash-landed onto **Heswall** Golf Club course 17 June 1926 - the River Dee side of the railway line. His life was saved by using a parachute and he became the first British member of the Caterpillar Club whose membership was open to those whose lives had been saved by a parachute*[HGC]

Above: *St Fillan's Preparatory School for Boys was the last house on the left in Riverbank Road **Lower Heswall** going towards the River Dee. It dated back to at least 1912 when Miss EC Gore [who sent this postcard] was the Principal. A Mrs Nicholls was Principal in 1930 and by 1939 Captain J Deedes was the Headmaster - it closed shortly after. The photograph was taken from what is now the car park at the bottom of Riverbank Road [see below]*

Below: *This was the Green Dormitory of St Fillan's Preparatory School Riverbank Road **Heswall** [see above]. One of its famous pupils was Philip Yorke of Erdig Hall near **Wrexham** North Wales who was here c.1912 before going on to Moorland House School [see 1904]. The school was in a healthy, but isolated position close to the River Dee with its bracing winds. After the Second World War it became the Margaret Bevan Home [see 1948]*

Above: *In the early hours of the morning Police Constable Mullins, who was on duty in Station Road **Lower Heswall**, saw flashlights along the railway line towards **Thurstaston**. Upon investigating he found three men with the railway station safe which had been ripped open. The men ran off leaving most of the safe contents behind but the constable gave chase and succeeded in catching and overpowering one of them. However, the other two returned and struck the constable several times with heavy weapons and he was eventually rendered unconscious. They dragged him to the platelayer's cabin and handcuffed him with his own handcuffs, then tied him up with rope, leaving him unconscious. After about half an hour he regained consciousness, freed himself and struggled across the railway line to Mr Guy Kellet's house Hill View who then administered first-aid and took him to the Police Station about a mile away - it is not known whether the robbers were later arrested*

Above: *The new **Heswall** Golf Club pictured here, which was built in 1925, replaced the one destroyed by fire in 1924 [see 1905]. It was designed by Herbert Rowse, a member of the club and erected in front of the site of the old building, which then provided a car park behind*[HGC]

PARKGATE SALT WATER BATHS

Open Middle of May to first Sunday in October, 9 a.m. to 9 p.m. Sundays only. Two sessions 9 a.m. to 1-15 & 2-15 to 9 p.m.
Mixed Bathing daily. Sundays included.

MAIN BATH 335½ ft long 50 ft. wide   SHALLOW BATH 220 ft long 60
depth 3½ ft. to 8 ft.   ft. wide, depth 2½ ft. to 4½ ft.
This bath makes bathing safe for all.

350 Dressing Boxes and large Changing Rooms. Spacious Sun Bathing
Decks free to bathers. Diving Stages, Spring Boards, Refreshment Buffet

Single Bathe	Adults 1/-	Juvenile under 16 6d.		Huge
Monthly Contract	„ 15/-	„ „ „ 10/-		Vita-Glass
Season Contract	„ 42/-	„ „ „ 30/-		Sun Bathing
Book of 24 tickets [Transferable] 21/-	„ „ „ 10/6			Pavilion free to bathers

Spectators 3d. each   Saturday, Sunday & Bank Holiday 6d.
Season 10/- Free Motor Park and large Picnic Field for bath visitors only
Accommodation for 1000 cars at owner's risk.
Come and spend a pleasant day, bring your own food if you like
or Bath Buffet will supply you if you prefer.
Frequent change of water, one bath always available during entire cleaning out of the other.
Motor pump replacing water at the rate of 3200 gallons per minute.
The Management will appreciate your interest in handing this card to a friend.

1927

- Thingwall Garage established in Barnston Road **Thingwall** [see 1930]
- A men's club was opened in **Barnston**, opposite the church, by Lord Leverhulme [see 1936]SOUV

Mar 12 The Colliery at **Little Neston** closed [see photo]N

May 16 Last remaining part of *Dawpool* **Thurstaston,** the former mansion of the Ismay family, was dynamitedNEWS

Above: *The 10 miners, who were pictured leaving the last shift before the Wirral Colliery at **Little Neston** closed down, were from left to right: Arthur Jones, Dave Parry, Joe Burkey, Joe Millington, Bill Williams, Richie Williams, John M Williams, Jack Campin, Henry Williams and 'Cobber' Jim Jones [obviously a Welsh influence]. The workings and slag heaps were left for many years [see 1957]*

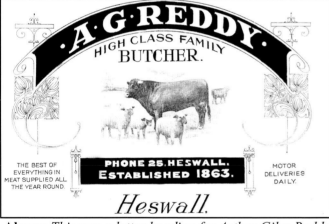

Above: *This was a letter heading for Arthur Giles Reddy who was a butcher in Pensby Road **Heswall** - his family had started the business in 1863*

Above: *Murrayfield School for Girls is seen in South Drive **Heswall** [see below]. A "Schools of England" book for parents describes the school thus: "Principals are Miss Whittall and Miss Henderson. Girls are taken from six to 15 years as boarders or daily pupils. Heswall is a most healthy place with the school situated on a hill above the River Dee and a great point is made of open-air exercise. There is ample space for games - tennis and cricket in summer with netball and lacross in winter. There is a flourishing school company of Girl Guides and a Brownie pack". The school closed in c.1972 when Mrs E Thomas was headmistress and the site was initially to become a new BUPA hospital with funds raised for the project. The site was not big enough and the former **Thingwall** Sanitorium was used [see 1929]. However, the name Murrayfield was used as the name of the new Hospital in Thingwall which opened in 1982 and the school's honours boards are on display there*

Below: *This postcard of the dining room of Murrayfield School [see above] was sent in 1927 by Miss Whittall, the Principal of the school, to a former pupil who had recently moved to Howell's School Denbigh*

Left: *This was a view of Sandy Lane **Irby** Mill Hill with Quarry Farm on the right - which was so named due to the now disused quarry at the back of the farmhouse and can be seen from the National Trust land. Joseph Smith was the farmer at the time who built the wooden holiday cottages which were initially let out and then some sold to those who rented them. There are a few still in use today*

73

– The Institute, **Little Neston** demolished - an extension to Neston Cottage Hospital built on the site[YW1]

Feb 11 Public electricity supply switched on at **Neston** for first time. A private works to supply specific areas had been built in 1908[N]

Dec 40 bungalows built in **Neston** [*Mayfield Gardens*][N]

Dec 24 *Kings Picture House* opened in Telegraph Road **Heswall** - seated 900 [see 1921][TSSW]

Above: The Roscote *is seen in Wall Rake* **Lower Heswall** *- one of its walls fronted onto Village Road opposite* Stacey's Cottage [see 1922]. *It was the the country home of Thomas Brocklebank, banker and member of the Liverpool shipping family. The building had been altered and enlarged c.1893 by Doyle. This splendid looking building was demolished and houses in Roscote Close were built on the site in the 1960s*

Above: Shore *or* Coastguard's Cottages *stood on the shoreline of the River Dee at* **Thurstaston**. *One of the cottages was also known as* Sally's Cottage *named after Sally McCrae who sold teas and refreshments from here between the wars. The large sandstone slabs leaning against the wall were probably from the quay or sea wall which was erected at* **Dawpool** [*see page 59*]. *More recently the cottages have been renovated and converted into one six bedroom residence*

Above: *The* Dee View Inn **Heswall** *is seen on the right looking down Dee View Road towards* **Lower Heswall** [see 1893]

Above: *This view of Lower Thingwall Lane* **Thingwall** *is unrecognisable today as both Woodfinlow Terrace on the left and* Thingwall Farm *on the right have been demolished*[Tv]

Above: *This was a comic postcard from* **Parkgate**

- A second bath opened at **Parkgate** open-air baths [see 1932][N]
- *Church House* High Street **Neston** demolished - the Parish Hall was built on the site[YW1]
- Dee Shellfish Company which was sited next to the *Boat House* **Parkgate**, investigated ways of preserving shellfish which could then be sent by post. The company ceased in 1931[N]

Right: *The Neston and Parkgate Hygenic Laundry and Cleaning Company was formed in 1896 on the site of the Deeside Electric Works at **Neston** [see 1882]. By 1914 they were employing 80 people when it was considered an alternative for girls to going into service. It was taken over by **Tranmere** Laundry in 1940. This was an interior view[N]*

Above: *Looking down School Hill **Heswall** from the top of Dee View Road with the tower of St Peter's Church silhouetted against the River Dee and Welsh hills beyond. The six terraced cottages on the right are still there today. The nearest one on the right, with a Cadbury's Chocolate sign in the window, being a shop then owned by Victor Hamilton, which was popular with children from the school further down the road*

Above: *The old **Irby** village has just started to be developed with the newly-built Constantine's Irby Stores on the left selling quality groceries and provisions. This was built by Arthur Constantine formerly of Rookery Farm for his son Kenneth. Three other shops were built adjoining Irby Stores [see 1936]. The former Prince of Wales Inn is seen on the right*

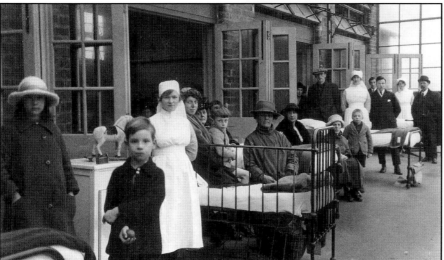

Above: ***Thingwall** Sanitorium was erected by The County Borough of **Birkenhead** with work commencing in 1922 [see below]. The Heswall area was considered very healthy and could be an aid in making ill children better. There were several children's homes in the area*

Left: *This was one of the boys' ward at **Thingwall** sanitorium - boys and girls were not allowed to mix. The name Murrayfield for the new BUPA Hospital built on this site came from Murrayfield School [see 1927] - the new hospital opened here in 1982*

1929 continued

Above: The Old Mill Cafe and Stores *is seen from Mill Hill Road* **Irby** *looking towards Mill Lane which led to* **Greasby** *- Arrowebrook Lane was to the right and Hill Bark Road to the left [a roundabout now stands in the middle of the road].* The cafe was orignally the *Miller's Cottage to the windmill which once stood to the left up Hill Bark Road [see 1897]. The cottage was purchased in 1919 by George and Bertha Lunsden who opened it as* The Old Mill Cafe *but was known locally as* Lumsden's Cafe. *Being at a crossroads and near to Irby Hill, it was very popular with walkers and cyclists. They served refreshments during the day but also held dances two or three evenings a week. In 1938 the property was purchased by Higson's Brewery of* **Liverpool**. *They applied several times over the years to demolish the cottage and build a new pub on the site. However, they were refused until 1978 when it was approved - but on condition that they retained the original cottage and any extensions had to be in keeping with this building.* The Mill *pub opened here in 1980*

Below: *The children are dressed for the Empire Day celebrations on 24 May 1930 at Dale Avenue Council School* **Heswall**. *Jean Stafford is on the extreme left, Stella Miles fourth from right and P Prosser centre back*

Above: *Looking towards the River Dee and Welsh hills beyond, the houses can be seen in Riverbank Road* **Lower Heswall** *[top centre]. The Stationmaster's House for Heswall Station is the one to the left of the tall bush and is still there today. The row of railwaymen's cottages beyond have since been demolished*

1930

- The old Vicarage building in High Street **Neston**, which had become a school, was demolished - Irwins grocery shop was built on the site. It became a Tesco store after they took over Irwins in 1960[N]
- Two new open-air wards built on the river side of the Royal Liverpool Children's Hospital Telegraph Road **Heswall** - Andrew Gibson donated £15,000 towards the cost[SOUV]
- The Heswall Operatic Society production was *The Sorcerer*
- **Neston** UDC build 30 houses in Burton Road [Talbot Gardens][N]

Jul **Heswall** Children's Sports Day was held for the last time because the field in The Slack, which they had used for many years, was to be built upon[NEWS]

Above: *The boilerhouse chimney is seen standing on the site of the Wirral Colliery at* **Little Neston**. *The colliery closed down in 1927 but some of the buildings and workings were left standing for years and the slag heaps for even longer [see 1957]*

Left: *Harold Keates and Lilian Dodd are seen in the doorway of the Methodist Tin Chapel in Irby Hill Road* **Irby** *after their wedding on 31 October 1930. The reception was held across the road at Lilian Dodd's home -* Irby Hill Farm *[see right]*

Above: *Harold Keates and Lilian Dodd are seen walking down the footpath of Irby Hill Farm* **Irby** *after their wedding at the Methodist Chapel - which is seen in the background to the left of the farmhouse and in the photo to the left. Lilian Dodd was born at the farmhouse - where the first local primitive Methodist meetings were held by her parents in their farmhouse kitchen*

Above: *Looking up High Street* **Neston** *away from The Cross, the Post Office was the first building on the right. In the far distance was the Wesleyan Church at the junction with Park Street [see 1908]. The lighter coloured building further up the street on the left was once a public house called* The Vaults, *later it was known as* The Letters *which eventually became the* Neston Hotel - *closing down in 1931*

Above: *Christ's Church Barnston was built at a cost of £3,000 being consecrated 30 June 1871. The other church in the parish opened in Gills Lane* **Barnston** *1904 [see 1918]*

Above: *The lady driver of the car registration number CM9999 [a Birkenhead registration] has stopped for petrol at Thingwall Garage Barnston Road **Thingwall** when petrol was half a penny a gallon! The garage was established in 1927 and operated into the 1990s. The site is now occupied by houses*

Above: *Heswall Stores which is seen on the left in Village Road **Lower Heswall** was once owned by a Mr Pennington who was called 'snatch-em' by the children as he would always ask the children for payment first before handing them the sweets they were buying. However, he gave all the children in the school on School Hill an orange on Maunday Thursday. There is a sign on the front of the shop saying 'public telephone' - this would encourage people to enter the shop to make their call - public telephone boxes initially made of concrete were introduced in 1920 - but not here. The big building on the right was once Smallwood's Bakery [see 1926] - sacks of flour etc would be hoisted up to the upstairs door on the left[YW6]*

Right: *The caption read 'Earle's Drive Neston'. The road was built in 1903 between Parkgate Road and Leighton Road and was named* Leighton Park Estate *by the builder NA Earle - there was never historically a* Leighton Park *- but was a name invented by the builder. The land here was once part of Neston Park, a medieval deer park. By the early 1930s there were eight houses in this straight tree-lined road. The land to the right is now Woodlands Road, where housing development took place in the 1960s[YW6]*

Above: *The front entrance to the* Hotel Victoria *is seen from Gayton Road **Lower Heswall** which was opened in 1902. It was owned by Bents Brewery who also owned the* Heswall Hotel *which later became the* Black Horse Hotel *the other end of Lower Heswall. The hotel was demolished in its centenary year 2002 and luxury housing built on the site*

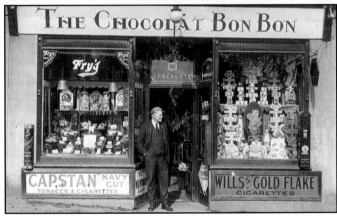

Above: *The Chocolate Bon Bon was a chocoholic's dream. Situated in Pensby Road **Heswall** near the junction with Telegraph Road, most of the window display however, was for cigarettes and also a Wild Woodbine machine above the Will's Gold Flake cigarette advert on the right. On the other side, above the Capstan Navy Cut cigarette sign, was a Pascal Pear Drops one penny machine. There was a Wrigley's machine in the doorway*

1931

- **Birkenhead** Corporation acquired the **Neston** and **Parkgate** Gas Company[N]
- *Neston Hotel* High Street **Neston** closed [see 1930][N]
- Dawstone Park was opened in **Heswall**[SOUV]

Above: The Fox and Hounds ***Barnston,*** *pictured here, was built in 1910 when this building replaced the original one which appeared in records of 1850 when John Sutton was the victualler [see page 22]*

Above: This was the long wooden slide at Dale House Farm ***Barnston*** *which was one of the most popular attractions at the Barnston Camp [see 1925]. The slide is mostly covered in - this was probably to protect the wood from the weather when out of season and removed when in use. The other attractions included swing boats, a large rotating swing, galloping horses on a Merry-go-round etc and 15 acres of fields and woods to play in [see 1925]*

JOHN HOUGH,

IRBY FARM, IRBY.

Pure New Milk. *Cream.* *New Laid Eggs.*

PRODUCER OF ACCREDITED MILK.
MOTOR DELIVERIES TWICE DAILY.

Left: *These four shops on the left in Thingwall Road **Irby** were built in the late 1920s with the building beyond being* Rookery Farm *[see page 63]. Shops were built on the right in the distance in 1937*

*Above: The thatched cottage adjoining the smithy, which was said to have dated back to 1604, once stood in Dawstone Road **Heswall** at the bottom of what is now Sandstone Walk. Billy Barlow was the last smith, who retired in 1964. One of his ancestors is reputed to have shod William III's horse when visiting Gayton Hall in 1689. The last few years that he worked here, with few horses to shod, he made ornamental wrought iron items to order*

Above: *Mickwell Brow **Ness**, the house on the horizon, was built by **Liverpool** Cotton Merchant Arthur Bulley in 1898. His hobby was gardening and developed part of his garden as a commercial nursery*

- The front wall [facing the Dee] of Mostyn House School **Parkgate** strengthened with a black and white facade [see 1933][N]
- **Brimstage** Village Hall erected on the site of the *Red Cat Inn*[YWPH]
- The *Devon Doorway* Restaurant opened in **Gayton** for a Mrs Aldridge who came from Devon [see 1940][YW1]

Above: *The tide is out with many boats seen on the beach at **Parkgate**. Looking across The Parade the Clontarf Cafe is on the right with the Red Lion Hotel next door before it was renovated and had the Worthington Warrington Ales sign hung above the door*

Above: *The ladies on the left are looking down on the beach at **Thurstaston** with Sally's Cottage being the white cottage seen close to the shoreline [see 1928]. The cliffs have eroded here over the years but despite this there are still holiday homes sited here with wonderful elevated views of the River Dee*

Right: *John Pride was a local artist and poet in the 1930s. This postcard entitled Emma Lyon, was a poem about one of her admirers when she was a young girl in **Ness** who saw her in London when she was Lady Hamilton [this is not accurate as she left Ness at a very young age]. She became Lord Nelson's lover [see 1865]. The etching is of **Parkgate** in the 1700s*

Above: *This was a view of Burton Road at **Ness** Holt with Fossel Bank the half-timbered building on the right at the junction of School Lane to the right and Dawn Close, a recent development, to the extreme right - both off picture. The rear entrance to Wyncote is on the left*

Above: *This view shows how popular **Thurstaston** Hill was in the 1930s with ramblers and a meeting place for sporty cars owners on the left and motor bikers on the right. There are probably 200 people seen at various parts of the hill on this postcard view taken by H Wragg of **Hoylake***

Above: *The boys are queueing at **Thurstaston** Camp which was owned and run by Lever Bros for their employees. Opening in 1921 it was also used as a treat for under privileged children including Charles Thompson's Mission **Birkenhead**. The camp was sited the river side of Thurstaston Station with accommodation in army huts which could sleep 90 men and 60 women - later family accommodation was made aavailable. They had wonderful views of the River Dee looking across to North Wales and activities included tennis, cricket, football and dancing. The camp closed at the outbreak of the Second World War and was taken over by the military, then becoming an anti-aircraft battery in 1941*

PARKGATE SWIMMING BATHS

Free Car Park for 1,000 Cars

400 Dressing Boxes

Sunbathing Deck & Vita-Glass Shelter

Additional Safety Bath for Beginners

Spectators

CAFE

Mixed Bathing 7 days weekly

Moderate Charges

THE BATHS, PARK GATE

Above: *This was a multi-view postcard of **Parkgate** swimming baths which were built on land purchased by AG Grenfell of Mostyn House School in 1922. The swimming bath, which opened 12 May 1923, was 335ft. long and 50ft. wide with the deep 'end' being in the middle. In 1930, a second bath was built on the Dee side - this was a shallow paddling pool for children and non-swimmers. Initially the baths were fed from the high tide but when this was not possible, a pump with filter was used. The baths were sold at auction in 1939 and kept open until 1942 when they closed. They reopened after the war but due to the River Dee silting up and the high cost of bringing water in by pipe, they closed c.1950. **Neston** Council bought the site in 1959 but it was not until 1974 that a picnic site and car park were built here for the Wirral Country Park [see advert above]*

1933

- New Urban District of **Neston** now included both **Ness** and **Burton**[N]
- **Burton's** annual flower show was revived after a gap of 12 years - also included sports, side shows, tennis and bowls[NEWS]

Feb The 'giant' square 140ft. chimney stack on the site of the old Wirral Colliery at **Little Neston** was demolished - the bricks were to be used as foundation stones for 'Home Crofts' which was an undertaking by the Neston Housing Society to build and let the new houses to the unemployed who were also given land on which to grow their own food[NEWS]

Apr Wirral Urban District Council formed[SOUV]

Aug **Irby** & District Social Club opened in Thingwall Road in the old *Rookery Farm* house[YW6]

Oct 8 "Whitfield Common **Heswall** presented to the Wirral Urban District Council by William Hulme 2nd Viscount Leverhulme 8 October 1933" - these details can be seen inscribed on a granite boulder on the common

Above: *Burton Village Hall was erected for the residents of* **Burton** *and* **Puddington** *in 1906 by Henry Gladstone, who then owned the village of Burton - he also gave them a considerable amount of the surrounding land. The hall, which was centre of village activity, was enlarged between the wars and the stage was added after the Second World War. It is still at the centre of activity today*

Above: *This photograph was taken from a panoramic postcard of Mostyn House School The Parade* **Parkgate** *in 1933. The buildings had been strengthened a year earlier with a new facade, being finished off with the imposing half-timbered effect, when the school buildings fronting onto the River Dee were in danger of collapsing*

Left: *This aerial photograph of* **Neston** *town centre shows the* New Cinema *in Chester Road bottom left; St Mary and St Helen Church top left in High Street; from The Cross in the centre to the top was Parkgate Road, leading towards* **Parkgate;** *the road leading from The Cross towards and then under the railway line bottom right was Brook Street. Halfway down Brook Street and to the right became the car park and open-air Market. The railway [bottom centre] which was the London and Northern Eastern Railway line travelling north to south from* **Bidston** *to* **Wrexham** *via Hawarden Bridge, which became British Railways in 1948, still operates today*

Above: *By 1933 the* Dee View Inn *Heswall in the centre of the photograph, with Dee View to the left and The Mount to the right, had become a Birkenhead Brewery pub. The shops on the right are in the background when crowds are walking towards the unveiling of the war memorial [see 1924]*

Right: *An advert for the Birkenhead Brewery pub the* Dee View Inn *Heswall - when JP Morewood was the proprietor [see photo above]*

Left: *This was view of the main gates to* **Thurstaston** *Hall [see 1920]*

Right: *These pensioners from Birkenhead are enjoying a day out at Dale House Farm Storeton Lane* **Barnston** *organised by Charles Thompson's Mission Hemingford Street* **Birkenhead**. *Although the farm catered mainly for families and children, the pensioners would enjoy watching the children and would be served afternoon tea in the tea room behind*

Left: *Elm Stores is seen facing Thingwall Road* **Irby** *with Mill Hill Road straight ahead. The stores were named after the very tall elm tree in front of the shop. This was Irby's second shop after the Post Office and run for many years by Mr Matthews [see 1926]. Mill Hill Road and Manor Road [first left down Mill Hill Road] were both made one-way streets 15 November 1935*

1934

- Plans to convert *Heswall* Castle into Council offices came to nothing mainly due to the cost of making the flat roof waterproof
- **Neston** Urban District Council bought the Town Hall Company for £4,500 - built extension for new Council Chamber in 1935[N]
- A lady was killed when a car overturned on the *Glegg Arms* corner **Gayton**[NEWS]
- A **Neston** man who was locked out of his house by his wife because he refused to pay her housekeeping, was ordered by the magistrates to pay £1 per week plus 5/- for each of his two children out of his wage of £3.12.6![NEWS]

Aug The existing camp on a four acre site on Broad Lane **Heswall** was purchased by the Liverpool Boys Association for £1,900 [see 1937][NEWS]

Above: *This was an advert for the* Green Shutter Cafe *The Parade* **Parkgate** *- which not only served afternoon teas, morning coffee, light luncheons, home made cakes in the garden tea house but was also a guest house [see photo below]*

Above: *The building with ivy growing up the side was the* Green Shutter Cafe *which stood on The Parade* **Parkgate** *[see advert above]. The building was the* Talbot Inn *between at least 1764 and 1808 - it is said that Mrs Fitzherbert, wife of George III stayed here to enjoy the sea air in c.1798. The building beyond with the bay windows was Prospect House which has probably always been a private residence. The black and white buildings beyond belonged to Mostyn House School [see 1933][TP]*

Dee Park Estate, Gayton, Wirral.

This Estate is now being developed and Detached or Semi-Detached Houses or Bungalows will be built to suit purchasers. Views of Dee Estuary and Welsh Mountains. Tenure Freehold—no road making charges. Building sites may be inspected by appointment.

Prices from £750

SOLE AGENT

ARTHUR M. BROWN, F.A.I.

43, CASTLE STREET,   LIVERPOOL

Telephone : BANK 4766 and HESWALL 273.

Above: *This was an advert for the Dee Park Estate* **Gayton** *where the properties would be built to suit the purchaser with prices starting at £750*

Above: *The Church of St Nicholas* **Burton** *was rebuilt in 1721 with the window in the north-east corner being 14th century. The church was unusual in that it only had an hour but no minute hand on the church clock - which dated back to c.1750*

Above: *Two shops have been added to Constantine's* **Irby** *Stores seen in 1929 and a further one was to be added [see 1936]. The former* Prince of Wales Inn *which had become private residences is seen on the right. It was to serve as the Irby Home Guard headquarters during the Second World War, being demolished in the 1950s and the site became a car park for the shops. The thatched single-storied Post Office, which is seen to the left of the car, lost its thatched roof in the 1950s and became the doctor's surgery [see 1950]*

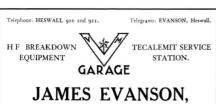

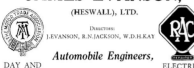

Above: *This was a view of Neston Mill Leighton Road **Neston** during its neglected years. The mill was last worked in the 1880s with the Gray family running a haulage, saw mill, wheelwright and smith business from the old mill yard [see 1952]*

Left: *The caption on this postcard read: 'Mrs Robert's Tea Rooms **Thurstaston**'. The tea rooms were at the back of* Hillside Farm *School Lane, which is seen on the left, where Mrs Robert's husband was the farmer. The tea rooms were very popular with church groups, ramblers and picnicers [see 1923]. School Lane disappears into the distance where it joined Thurstaston Road at the* Heatherlands Cafe

Above: *The shops on the left in **Lower Heswall** village were from the left: LE Drew, fruiterer and florist; Brierley, stationer and tobacconist; Heswall Post Office with a sign for public telephone above the entrance and Lloyds Bank in what was formerley Smallwood's Bakery. The Lydiate was to the right of the vehicle in the distance*

1935

- *Dee House* on the Parade **Parkgate** demolished - Nicholls' Cafe and Ice Cream Parlour and a shop either side opened on the site [see 1953][N]
- **Heswall** Castle demolished [see 1906]

Apr 17 The Wirral Harriers held their Point-to-Point meeting at *The Oaks Farm* **Ledsham** [see photo next page][TCHWH]

Jun 15 The **Liverpool** Ramblers' Association organised an open-air meeting with speakers at Thor's Stone **Thurstaston** to make the public aware of the countryside [see photo][WM]

Nov 15 Mill Hill Road and Manor Road **Irby** were made one-way streets[NEWS]

Above: *Burton* Post Office not only supplied the locals with their facilities but also ramblers and others visiting the village to admire its beauty and quaintness. The advertising boards on the left are for Park Drive and Gold Flake cigarettes - how times have changed!

Above: St Nicholas House **Burton**, *the three-storied building on the right, was built in 1711. It became the official vicarage in the 19th century until 1911 [see 1912]. Church House is seen between the two poles [see 1904]*

Above: *A meeting was organised by the Ramblers' Association at Thor's Stone **Thurstaston** Hill on 25 June 1935 to call public attention to the need for preserving the countryside; granting increased access to the mountains and the moorlands of the country and protecting existing footpaths and providing additional paths. The speakers were:- Rev HH Symonds; Miss AL Bulley [**Ness** Gardens] TG Pinder and Chairman H Graham White MP[WM]*

Above: *This was the entrance to **Heswall** Boys' Camp in Broad Lane at the bottom of Delavor Road **Heswall**. Opened in 1934, this four acre site belonged to the Merseyside Youth Association [see 1959]*

Left: *The last two estates on this Boulton's Sunshine Villas advert were one of the lowest and highest cost - Station Road **Heswall** which then cost from £620 or 14/7d per week [62.5p per week] and Chester Road **Gayton** cost from £975 or 22/9d per week [£1-13.5p per week]. House prices rose after the Second World War from 1946 so these properties were a good buy*

Left: *The gates are seen at the entrance to* **Thurstaston** *Hall which dated back to 1070 The hall is unusual in that it has never been offered for sale as it has been passed down the same family, sometimes by bequest through a godson, from generation to generation[YW6]*

Above: *The Wirral Harriers, who hunted both fox and hare, are seen passing through* **Burton** *woods. The pack, which was founded in 1868 by Mr John R Court, had 20 couples of small foxhounds in kennels at* **Puddington***. In the 1930s the pack hunted on Tuesdays, Thursdays and Saturdays with the subscription being £40 a season with a cap of £2 per day [see 1909][TCHWH]*

Right: *The house on the right was Sven Tor [see 1913] in Pipers Lane* **Lower Heswall***. The houses on the near left were in Sandfield Park with the railway line behind running from left to right. In the distance, the other side of the line on the left, was Banks Avenue with Mostyn Avenue in the centre [see 1938]*

Above: *Looking down Holmwood Avenue* **Thingwall**

1936

- Presbyterian Church of England Telegraph Road **Heswall** purchased 1,140 sq. yds. of land formerly part of *Heswall Castle* Grounds[YW6]
- Wirral Urban District Council purchased *Hill House* Rocky Lane **Heswall** together with five acres of land [see 1959][SOUV]
- *Castle Building* row of shops in Telegraph Road **Heswall** opened for business[YW1]
- The **Liverpool** Boys' Association purchased an additional six acres of farm land adjoining their camp in Broad Lane **Heswall** in 1934. There were many youth clubs affiliated to the Association who used the camp over the years[NEWS]

Mar   Christ's Church **Barnston** was lit by electricity for the first time - previously used oil lamps[SOUV]

Sep 17   Irby Methodist Church opened in Mill Hill Road **Irby** - built by Cartwright Brothers of Little Sutton at a cost of £6,100 - prior to this they used the tin chapel opposite Irby Hill Farm [see 1930][YWPH]

Above: Irby Hill Farm *is behind the trees on the right in Irby Hill Road* **Irby** *[see 1930]. The road was straightened and widened here in the 1980s with the bend in the road to the right now being the slip road in front of Irby Cricket Club.* Hill Cottage *is seen in the distance*

Above: *The fourth and final shop has been added to the row in Thingwall Road* **Irby** *[see 1934]. The former* Prince of Wales Inn *which had become private residences is seen on the right and was to become the centre for the Irby Home Guard during the Second World War. The building was demolished in the 1950s and the site is now a car park for the shops [see 1929 and 1934]*

Above: *George Nickson's recovery vehicle from Burton Garage, Chester High Road* **Burton** *is attending an accident on the Chester High Road. A car is being towed out of the ditch with the aid of several willing helpers. This is an enlarged photograph taken from a blotting pad advert [see below]*

Above: *This advert for George Nickson's from Burton Garage and Petrol Filling Station Chester High Road* **Burton** *was in the form of a blotting pad. This lists all his services available and includes a photograph of his vehicle rescuing a car from the ditch [see enlarged photo above]*

Above: *This was Nicholls' Model Dairy shop in Brook Street **Neston** - the milk came from their Ashfield Farm Dairy which was owned by Mr WK Nicholls. They also opened Nicholls' milk bar and ice cream parlour on The Parade **Parkgate**. They were awarded a diploma in ice cream at the 1935 Olympia and have been winning national awards ever since. Nicholls' Ice Cream is still as popular today and a visit to Parkgate would not be complete without one of their famous ice creams*

Above: *This was an advert for Leeman's Garage on The Parade **Parkgate** [see photo below]*

Right: *A high tide is seen looking along The Parade **Parkgate** with Leeman's garage on the left [see advert above] in front of the half-timbered cafe -which is a restaurant today. The car on the left is by the turning into Mostyn Square*

Above: *There is a high tide at **Parkgate** with fishing boats seen in the distance. Mostyn Square is off to the right. Behind the tall flag pole was the Convalescent Home and to the right of it Leeman's Garage [see advert above]*

- **Chester** Co-op Society built new premises on the site of their existing shop in **Neston**[N]
- Gould's opened their new printing and stationery branch at 3 Castle Buildings **Heswall** and are probably one of the only businesses from then still trading in Heswall today[SOUV]
- c.1935 Nicholls' Milk Bar and Ice Cream Parlour opened on The Parade **Parkgate**. It was very controversial at the time as it was a very modern building. It consisted of a six bedroom house at the back, three shops at the front:- Grace Brooke and Bensons were either side of Nicholls' Cafe where where was access to the balcony from inside the shop from which there were wonderful views of the River Dee and beyond [see 1953]
- The old sandstone *Corner House Farm* **Irby** was demolished [the site is now Broster's yard] - also in **Irby** a new block of shops was built on the south side of Thingwall Road[WBB]

May 12 Coronation Day for King George VI and Queen Elizabeth. Events were held on the day within the Wirral Urban District to celebrate the occasion [see details below]

May 17 Coronation Gymkhana held at **Heswall** Football ground including not only horse events but also fun ones including:- Errand boys' cycle race; pillow fight; blindfold boxing; crooning and bun eating competitions[SOUV]

Jun 12 Coronation Regatta and Swimming Gala held opposite the Dee Sailing Club **Thurstaston**

Oct 17 Bruce Ismay of **Thurstaston** [Chairman of White

Events organised within the Wirral Borough Council on Coronation Day included:

A Coronation Beacon was lit on Poll Hill **Heswall** - this was one of a chain of beacons throughout the country - followed by fireworks organised by 1st Heswall Scout Troop; Bonfire and fireworks at *Irby Hill Farm;* **Irby** and **Thurstaston** athletic sports for boys and girls held on ground adjoining Irby Hall Farm; Athletic sports for school children of **Barnston, Heswall**, **Gayton** and **Pensby** held at Heswall AFC football ground Barnston Road with a gymnastic display by the Heswall Nautical Training School - all school children in the area received a Coronation Beaker

Above: *Taken from Costain's brochure for their development at Parkway* **Irby** *[see right and 1960]*

Above: *Looking along Gayton Road* **Lower Heswall -** White Lodge *is the house on the right on the corner of Wall Rake which was once the* White Lion *[see 1902]; Behind the wall in the centre was* The Roscote *[see 1928]; the white building opposite was* Stivelooms *on the corner of Station Road and on the site to the left of the trees was once* 'Tiger' Smith's Cottage *[see 1924]*

Above: *The* Anchor Inn *was situated in Thurstaston Road opposite Thingwall Road* **Irby**. *The back portion of the cottage was the original and said to probably be 17th century. There was an inn mentioned in Irby in Elizabethan days but the location was not known.[T] This dates back as an inn to at least 1822 when Edward Howard was the victualler. Birkenhead Brewery bought the inn at auction in June 1940 for £12,000. The outbuildings to the right were later demolished and the site is now the car park*

FREEHOLD £795 . 0 . 0 inclusive

No road charges, legal costs or other extras beyond the advertised price
Built by
R. COSTAIN & SONS (LIVERPOOL) LTD
House Builders for over 70 years

Above: *Advert for Costain's development at Parkway* **Irby** *[see left and 1960]*

Above: The Stores *was a grocers shop owned by Bernard Steel in Mill Lane* **Ness**. *Most of the adverts in the window are for cigarettes - Wills' Capstan, Wills' Star, Wills' Gold Flake and Players Please with a board outside the shop for Wills' Star*

Above: *Muriel Boumphrey, the author's mother, is seen standing outside* Floreat *1, Glenwood Drive* **Irby**, *after her wedding. The cost of the house then - including charges - was £817*

Above: *Ploughing the fields with horses was still used by some Wirral farmers into the 1950s - seen here in the 1930s on Church Farm* **Thurstaston**. *A team of horses could only manage three quarters of an acre a day whereas a tractor could plough many fields in the same time. The ploughing would take place in winter - there are no leaves on the trees - and would be ploughed with the lay of the land, so water would be naturally drained off down the furrows.*[Tv] *The spire of St Bartholemew's Church* **Thurstaston** *can be seen in the distance*

Right: *This was an advert for the Coronation Gymkhana held on Whit Monday at* **Heswall** *Football ground Barnston Road*

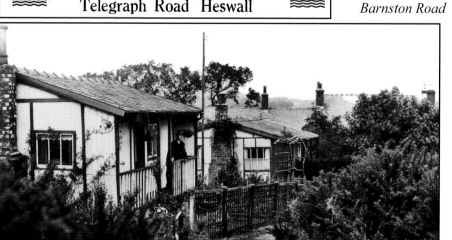

Left: *The caption on the postcard read: "Pretty Bungalows, Irby Mill Hill". They were wooden holiday cabins on* **Irby** *Heath, built on land belonging to* Quarry Farm *- the roof in the background belonged to* Irby Hill Farm *in Hill Bark Road*

1938

–   New wooden clubhouse for the Dee Sailing Club opened at **Heswall**[SOUV]

–   Higson's Brewery bought *Lumsden's Cafe* Mill Lane **Irby** - planning permission refused until the late 1970s. *The Mill* pub opened in 1980[YWPH]

Feb   A plaque was placed by the Quakers' Graves in **Burton** as a tribute to the men and women who adopted a courageous attitude in difficult times [see 1904][NEWS]

Jun 6   The men's club in **Barnston**, opposite the church, was burnt down[SOUV]

Oct 15   **Irby** Village Hall opened in Thingwall Road - the freehold site was given by Miss L Lee Townsend [later Mrs Colley] and the hall built at a cost of over £2,000

Above: *Bathers and sun bathers are enjoying the sun at **Parkgate** Baths. Originally built for Mostyn House School Parkgate in 1923 but opened up to the public. Mr EG Grenfell sold the baths in 1939 and used the money to build air-raid shelters under the school. They closed in 1942 and opened for a few years after the war finally closing c.1950 [see 1932]*

Left: *The three people are crossing Pensby Road **Thingwall** - Sparks Lane is to the right of the photographer. The canopy of the last shop in the row is seen on the left with Penrhyn Avenue to the left of the further car*

Right: *The people on the right are waiting at the bus stop in Pensby Road **Pensby** for the approaching Crosville bus route number 114 which had a destination board **Heswall** via Pensby. The shops on the left, which were built in the 1930s included from the left:- RB Roots, chemist; Pensby Post Office; Hartleys, drapers; S Hutchesson*

Left: *Looking down Mostyn Avenue **Heswall** towards the River Dee, the Welsh hills are seen in the background. These houses, which were built by Jones and Hough of Heswall in 1927, were the first in Heswall to built using breeze blocks. They were mainly lived in by fishermen and with probably none of them having cars, the road was very narrow with no provision for garages. Mostyn Avenue, Banks Road and The Moorings were known as 'the bonks'[Tv]*

Above: *The* Boathouse Cafe *is viewed from the beach at* **Parkgate**. *Originally there was an inn on the site dating back to c.1664 with a daily ferry service operating from here to* **Flint** *and elsewhere. There was a coach from here to take ferry passengers to* **Birkenhead** *where they could catch the Mersey ferry to* **Liverpool** *and after 1840 to* **Hooton** *where they could link into the national railway system. By the time the inn was so badly damaged by a storm in 1885 that it had to be demolished it had become known as the* Pengwern Arms. *The only part of the inn remaining was the stables which were demolished in the 1960s and the site now forms part of the garage car park. The* Boathouse Cafe *was built on the site of the inn in 1926 - as seen here. In 1977 the building was enlarged and became a restaurant[TP]*

Above: *The fishermen are unloading their catch at the Middle Slip* **Parkgate** *onto a lorry where it would probably be taken to Parkgate station and then by rail to customers all over the country*

Above: *Very few people are braving the stormy weather at* **Parkgate** *- the photo was taken from outside the* **Red Lion** *whose sign can be seen top left*

Left: *The Cleveland petrol pump which belonged to Leeman's Garage is seen on the right with the* **Parkgate** Convalescent Home *behind - this building was used to house evacuee children during the Second World War but was later demolished.* Overdee *was the prominent building beyond and the* Boathouse Cafe *can be seen in the distance on the left*

– **Neston** Parish Church tower used as an observation post by the Neston Home Guard - with a wooden hut provided[N]

– New Police Section Headquarters built in Hinderton Road **Neston** [see 1948][N]

– Leighton School in Boathouse Lane **Parkgate**, which had been founded there in 1918, closed when May Richardson retired - it was then requisitioned by the military [see 1955][NW]

Jul Mostyn House School **Parkgate** built the largest air raid shelter in the district - being 100ft. long x 22ft. wide x 10ft. high which could hold 280 people without mechanical ventilation or 350 with. Costing over £2,500 it was paid for by selling the Parkgate swimming baths [see 1932][NW]

Aug 31 Four days before war broke out, the Minister of Health and Defence regulations delegated power to Wirral District Council to take possession of **Heswall** Golf Club. Evacuees arrived the following day and occupied the clubhouse. Limited golf continued to be played despite the club being required to graze sheep on the course[WHF]

Sep Lever Brothers' camp at **Thurstaston** closed at the outbreak of war - later used as an anti-aircraft battery as part of **Liverpool's** defences[YW6]

Sep 3 War Declared

Nov 4 Our Lady and St John Roman Catholic Church was blessed in Telegraph Road **Heswall**[SOUV]

WILLIAM FLEMING & CO.
(J. R. FLEMING)

Building Contractors & Decorators

Cross Street *and* Liverpool Road, NESTON

LEIGHTON HALL FREEHOLD ESTATE

Wirral's Super Building Estate

THREE HOUSES ON ESTATE AS ILLUSTRATED

Magnificent Views of the River Dee and Welsh Hills. Excellent Schools, Golf and Swimming Baths. Electric Light. Main Water and Main Drainage on the site.

For further particulars apply to the owners :

WILLIAM FLEMING & COMPANY
Cross Street, Neston

or to the Agents :

Boult, Son & Maples *and* Hughes & Jones
5, Cook Street   10 Grange Road   19, Hamilton Square
LIVERPOOL   WEST KIRBY   BIRKENHEAD

Above: *The three houses illustrated in this advert were from 'Wirral's Super Building Estate' - the Leighton Hall Estate - which were advertised as having: 'magnificent views of the River Dee and Welsh Hills, excellent schools, golf and swimming baths. Electric light, main water and main drainage on the site'*

Above: *The goods train on the Mid Wirral line is seen about to pass the **Heswall** Hills signal box probably carrying iron ore from Bidston Docks to John Summers' steelworks at Shotton. This was the last of the main lines to open in Wirral in 1896 - the Heswall Hills station opened in 1898*

Right: *Looking down Oldfield Drive **Heswall**. The fence on the left was the boundary for the Clever sanitorium [see 1920]. The new buildings in the distance were probably in the Broad Lane vicinity with the River Dee and Welsh hills in the distance*

Left: West Lyn *Nurseries dated back to 1921 when land in Pipers Lane **Heswall** was purchased, the bungalow built in 1923 and the nurseries opened with 7,500 sq. yds. of land. At this time there were only about 10 houses in Pipers Lane listed in Kelly's Directory*

Above: *Shotwick village is seen from the tower of St Michael's Church. This small hamlet had a population of under 100 in the 1930s - mostly connected with farming. The cottage facing the road with the dark gable end was once the* Greyhound Inn. *There was an inn mentioned in Shotwick as far back as 1561 [see 1887]. In former times Shotwick was an important place with a castle to keep the Welsh out [by the 17th century it was in a ruinous state and the only sign today is a mound], and, when the head of the River Dee silted up in the 13th century Shotwick became the point of embarkation for* **Chester**. *It is hard to visualise today that the Dee once came within a field west of the churchyard wall of Shotwick Church*THW

Above: *This was an advertising postcard for the newly opened 'Tudor Rose Country Club and Road House'. Situated close to the Welsh Crossroads - otherwise known as* **'Two Mills'** *- in June 1939 a provisional licence was granted for the new hotel* Tudor Rose *to Higson's Brewery [see Two Mills Garage 1953]*

Above: *The Birkenhead Brewery* Pensby Hotel *Pensby Road* **Pensby** *is seen here shortly before opening in 1939. This was a typical design of the brewery's public houses in the 1930s - the* Arrowe Park Hotel *and* Railway Inn *at Meols being others. The hotel was built to cater for the newly developing area in its vicinity and the facilities included four customary bars- parlour, lounge, public and buffet which served snacks and sandwiches. Upstairs there was a dining room for weddings and dinner parties and a smaller room for similar functions seated 50*WTDW

Above: *The customer is buying Parkgate shrimps from the wife of the fisherman that caught them - by having a table outside they were able to attract the attention of passers-by. Mealor's is the only shop in* **Parkgate** *still selling fresh fish*

Right: *The sign above the door of the* **Irby** *Post Office said 'Ye Olde Post Office'. A new telephone box is seen on the left with a cigarette machine to the right of the lady with a pram. Part of a small shop seen on the right, which had been built between the Post Office and Constantine's grocery shop, sold and repaired watches*

1940

– Leeman's Printers had been bombed out and moved from Water Street **Liverpool** to the less vulnerable **Neston** - Jack Leeman, who lived in Neston, kept his company there after the war ended - setting his business up in Leighton Road[NW]

May 4 New fire station opened Telegraph Road **Heswall** cost *c.*£14,000[YWPH]

May 10 Evacuation of Dunkirk

May 14 National Local Defence Volunteers formed

Jun The *Anchor Inn* **Irby** sold at auction - purchased for £12,000 by **Birkenhead** Brewery[YW6]

Jun Evacuees from Guernsey arrived at **Irby**[WHF]

Jul 7 Evacuees from Guernsey arrived at **Neston** via Manchester[NW]

Jul 23 LDV became known as the Home Guard

Jul 29 Some high explosive bombs were dropped over Wirral including **Neston, Thurstaston** and **Irby** leaving craters but no casualties[NW]

Aug 5 First Mass said in Our Lady of Pity Roman Catholic Church which opened in Mill Lane **Greasby** using an old army hut which had served Our Lady and St John **Heswall** since 1919[HDS]

Nov 16 A German Junkers 88, which had been shot down near **Bromborough** Dock, was displayed in a field off Bevyl Road **Parkgate** for a week where it raised money for the local Spitfire Fund[NW]

Above: *The snow covered* Devon Doorway *was built in the 1930s for a Devonshire lady Mrs Aldridge - at the junction of Chester High Road, Barnston Road, Well Lane and Telegraph Road* **Gayton**

Below: *Daisy Kendrick is sitting in a bomb crater in a field belonging to* **Irby** *Hill Farm - next to their farmhouse - which is now part of Irby Cricket Club's ground. The damage was caused on the night of the 21/22 December 1940, by a German bomber jettisoning its load when returning from an raid, which caused a lot of damage to the Birkenhead area. The main damage here was caused to Kendrick's* Hill Cottage *in Irby Hill Road - with no one injured. Damage was also caused by another bomb in Rylands Hey,* **Greasby**. *It became quite a landmark with many inquisitive people visiting the site*

Above: *This postcard, which was sent in 1940, shows the* Cosy Cafe *behind the cars on the left and next door was the* Red Lion. *This was the oldest surviving public house, dating back to at least 1822, which at one time was extended and today incorporates the former* Cosy Cafe

Left: *The* Heswall Hotel *[renamed the* Black Horse Hotel *in 1941], which is the half-timbered building centre left, is seen from St Peter's Church tower* **Lower Heswall**. *The washing on the line is in the garden of* Elder Cottage *which was opposite the hotel and demolished in the 1950s [see 1958]*

1941

– War Weapons Week raised £125,000 in the **Neston** area[NW]

Apr 15 Leighton School Boathouse Lane **Parkgate** was occupied by the 'Z' Company of the 9th Battalion Royal Northumberland Fusiliers[NW]

May 8 One of the crew of a German plane shot down after dropping its bombs over the **Liverpool** Docks, gave himself up coming up the slope by the Boathouse Cafe **Parkgate**. He was taken to the Home Guard guard room at Leighton School Boathouse Lane before being collected by the military police[NW]

May 31 Church School in School Hill **Lower Heswall** suffered major bomb damage and destroyed the house of Mr Loose the Headmaster [YW1]

Nov 21 2nd Lieutenant G Ward Gunn of **Neston** was killed in North Africa and awarded a posthumous VC [see this page]. An appeal in 1943 to endow a hospital bed in his name at **Little Neston** Cottage Hospital raised £1,562[NW]

On 21 November 1941 Second-Lt. George Ward Gunn was in command of a troop of four anti-tank guns, part of a battery of 12 guns attached to a rifle brigade column in Side Rezegh.

Under heavy fire from 60 enemy tanks, the battery was almost destroyed, in spite of Second-Lt Gunn's efforts to re-group and encourage his men. Eventually only two guns were left in action, and subjected to relentless fire. Immediately afterwards, one of these guns was blown up and the portee of the other set on fire. All the crew were wounded, except the sergeant, although the last gun remained undamaged.

Second-Lt Gunn ran to the emplacement through intense fire and put the gun into action on the burning portee, the sergeant acting as loader. Regardless of the concentrated enemy fire, Second-Lt Gunn's shooting was so accurate at a distance of 800 yards that at least two enemy tanks were hit and set on fire and three others were badly damaged.

At any moment the fire might have reached the ammunition with which the portee was loaded, but the two men fought on until Second-Lt Gunn fell dead, the victim of a stray bullet which shattered his forehead.

Second-Lt Gunn was awarded a posthumous VC

Left: *St Winefried's Roman Catholic Church **Neston** is pictured on the left in Burton Road [see 1910]. The Church Hall on the right, was a gift in 1902 of Roger Taylor of **Parkgate***

Above: *A member of the Home Guard is walking past a snow drift over 8ft. high in Thingwall Road **Irby***

Below: *Much of the snow seen above in **Irby** Village has been cleared from the road, causing problems for the shops*

Above: *On the night of 31 May 1941 a German bomber was hit by AA shells during a raid on Merseyside. It jettisoned its load which destroyed a row of houses in Village Road **Lower Heswall** - Mr and Mrs Shone and their daughter Dorothy were killed*

1942

– The Ministry of Health requisitioned 22 acres of land at Clayhill Liverpool Road **Neston** - by the end of the war 37 brick huts and 14 precast buildings were erected there. They were used as an army camp, then a clearing station for Gibraltians, in 1944 for evacuees from the flying bombs in London and by the Royal Navy [see December 1945][NW]

Mar National Warship Week - including towns in Wirral which collected money to sponsor warships including:- **Hoylake** raised £428,208 for HMS *Verdun*, Wirral [**Heswall** and District] raised £150,346 for HMS *Orphelia* and **Neston** raised £99,000 for a Motor Torpedo Boat[NEWS]

May 3 Death of Mr Arthur K Bulley founder of **Ness** Gardens [see text 1948]

Above: *This was the Rose Pergola at **Ness** Gardens on a postcard posted in 1944. During the Second World War to help the war effort, the gardens produced fruit and vegetables which were sold in **Neston**. The founder Mr Arthur Bulley died in 1942 and his daughter presented the gardens and house to Liverpool University in 1948[N] [see 1905]*

Above: *This was the patriotic shop window of Irwins grocery store in Pensby Road **Heswall** which was promoting the 'Salvage Ammunition for the Home Front'. The posters were reminding the public to save and not throw away. The poster on the left advertised: 'Waste Wanted for War Weapons - Paper Bones Metal Rags -This Week and Every Week, Salvage is Essential'. The middle poster asks for: 'Put Out Rags and Bones - They Make Glue for aircraft'. The third poster has a picture of a pig with the caption 'We Want Your Kitchen Waste'*

Below: *The other window in Irwins **Heswall** shop [see above] has further details for salvaging and the sign in Dewhurst's butcher shop on the right says: 'Rationing - You Are Respectfully Invited to Re-register Here'*

FOR
QUALITY in Groceries and Provisions
Telephone 116
PEARSON'S
Proprietors: COOPER & CO's STORES LTD
COFFEE ROASTED DAILY
BRIDGE STREET NESTON

Above: *Thurstaston Hill, to the left of the picture, was a popular venue. The Cottage Loaf is seen above where the road bends [see advert 1932]*

1943

- The Riverside Players were formed performing in the assembly Rooms Dee View **Heswall**[WHF]
- The railings from Puddydale School **Heswall** were removed for salvage[SOTP]

Aug 24 A Wellington bomber on a training flight from Moreton-in-Marsh crashed on the marshes near the *Harp Inn* **Little Neston** - two of the crew were injured[NW]

Oct 19 A bed at Neston Cottage Hospital **Little Neston** was unveiled in memory of 2nd Lieutenant G Ward Gunn MC - a local man who had been awarded a posthumous VC [see photo below and text 21 November 1941][NPR]

Nov Due to lack of war time labour - several boys from Puddydale School **Heswall** were excused school to pick potatoes[SOTP]

Above: *This was the most popular part of **Heswall** beach. Being at the bottom of Riverbank Road it was an easy walk down from Heswall Station which was at the top of the road. Although not many people are about, there were two people in the waters of the River Dee. The houses to the right of the flagpole were in Park West*

Left: *The single-storied newsagent's shop is on the right in **Little Neston** village. The building straight ahead was the Neston Cottage Hospital [see 1920]. During the early years of the Second World War the hospital was rumoured to be closing. However, it was saved due to the income received from evacuated patients. A bed was endowed in memory of 2nd Lieut. G Ward Gunn MC who was awarded a posthumous VC in 1941[NW]*

Above: *The policeman on duty in the middle of the road at the junction of Telegraph Road **Heswall**, with Pensby Road to the left and The Mount to the right, is not very busy! Due to petrol rationing most private vehicles were only driven occasionally. However, the 'stop me and buy one' ice cream seller on the right, in front of Lloyds Bank, did not have that trouble with his tricycle!*

1944

May 20 Start of Wirral UDC 'Salute The Soldier Week'. The district's target was £150,000 which would cover the cost of equipping and clothing three parachute battalions. Centres were at **Heswall, Barnston, Irby** and **Pensby**[SOUV]

Jun 6 **'D' Day landings in Normandy**

Aug Puddydale School **Heswall** took 38 evacuees from London and southern counties[SOP]

Sep 10 A Mosquito on a training flight from Shropshire crashed during an exercise on the bombing range at **Burton**, landing in a field off Snab Lane **Ness** - both crew were killed[NW]

Dec 31 **Neston** Home Guard stood down[NW]

Above: *The River Dee and Welsh Hills can be seen in the distance looking down Bull Hill **Little Neston**. The end two cottages on the left were once* The Bull and Dog Inn, *which dated back to at least 1822 but had closed by 1923, was converted into two private houses [see 1920]*

*Above: This and the picture below were two of a series of publicity photographs taken by the Ministry of War. Jack Grundy of 1 Parkway Close **Irby**, who was on a seven day privelege leave having served in Africa and Sicily, is photographed shopping in Irby Village with his wife Dorothy and children Gilda and Randall [see 1945].*
*Below: Jack Grundy and family [see photo above] are walking along **Thurstaston** Station platform in order to have Jack's photograph taken, saying farewell to his wife and family. The bridge in the background was for Station Road*

Right: *All the buildings here in Burton Road **Ness** were seen in 1903 with the exception of the new* Wheatsheaf Inn *seen in the left background. However, by 1960 all the thatched cottages had been demolished [see 1951]*

Left: *This was a side view of the* Old Quay House *at **Neston** in a derelict state. It dated back to 17th century when it was an inn until c.1710 when it became three dwellings. In 1750 it was leased to the County of Cheshire who used it as the Neston House of Correction to house Irish vagrants who were being deported to Dublin under the Poor Laws. It became a private house until c.1915 and was then derelict as seen here in the early 1940s. It was then used as target practice by the Home Guard and reduced to rubble*

1945

May 8 VE [Victory in Europe] Day celebrated - there was a march-past parade at **Hoylake** for all the local volunteer home defence services - **Neston** and **Hoylake** Town Halls were decorated with flags - there was also dancing into the early hours[WHF]

Jul Many of the evacuees from Guernsey who had been taken into Wirral homes, including **Heswall**, **Barnston**, **Neston** and **Irby** in June 1940 returned home[WHF]

Aug 6 First atom bomb dropped on Hiroshima Japan

Aug 9 Second atom bomb dropped on Nagasaki

Aug 14 Japan surrenders to the Allies

Aug 15 VJ [Victory in Japan] Day - end of war celebrations across Wirral - music by bands, floodlighting of public buildings, bonfires, parades, street parties - there was a march-past parade at **Hoylake** for all the local volunteer home defence services [WHF]

Dec School children at Puddydale School **Heswall** were given an extra two days holiday at Christmas as part of victory celebrations[SOTP]

Dec 3 A Royal Navy shore establishment HMS *Mersey* was set up at Clayhill Liverpool Road **Neston** - it closed in July 1946 and the buildings were then occupied by squatters. The Council refurbished the 50 buildings into three-bedroom dwellings to make them habitable - the rent was 12/6 per week [see 1947][NW]

Dec 18 The barmaid of the *Holywell Hotel* **Parkgate** was murdered in Wood Lane by a demobbed sailor James Palmer - he served nine years in prison[NW]

Above: *This row of six terraced houses called* Mealor's Cottages *stood in Well Lane off Neston Road* **Ness** *- they replaced a row of ancient thatched cottages [see 1898]. The gap between the walls on the left is now Well Close with a small housing development. The houses in the background were in Snab Lane*

Above: *Looking up Mill Lane* **Ness,** Dial Terrace *was on the left,* Laburnum Farm *straight ahead and opposite the farm was a small white thatched cottage. The cottage plus farm buildings on the right have since been demolished and modern houses built on the site*

Above: *The children are taking part in country dancing at Everleigh Prep School watched by proud parents. This private prep school at the top of Coombe Road* **Irby** *was run by a Mrs Ellis. The names on the back of this photograph include: Donald Morris, Joyce Studley, Randall Grundy [see previous page], Winifred Dalzell, Beryl Pope and Wendy Wilson*

1946

Jul 6   The licence of the *Red Lion Inn* **Parkgate** passed back to Malcolm Campbell, on his return after war duties, from his wife. She had become the licensee at the beginning of the war when Malcolm joined the Merchant Navy[NEWS]

Above: *The Woodlands Cafe, which also served petrol, was located on the Chester High Road at the junction of Dunstan Lane* **Burton**

Above: *The new tea pavilion is seen at Neston Cricket Club* **Parkgate**

Right: *This was a view of the* **Heswall** *Hills Station on the Bidston to North Wales line. The line opened in 1896 and this station opened 1 May 1898 and has remained open ever since [see below]*

Left: *The* **Neston** *Station was opened on the* **Bidston** *to North Wales line in 1896 [see above]. It later changed its name to Neston and Parkgate, then Neston North and when Neston South closed on the Hooton - West Kirby line in 1962 it became just Neston*

Left: *This post-war view of The Parade* **Parkgate** *shows some cars able to travel despite the petrol rationing. The 'firewood man' John Reeves, who has just passed in front of Nicholls' Cafe, is travelling by one of the best ways then - horse and cart*

1947

– Proposal to extend **Irby** Village Hall [see October 1938] - the floor space would be double the existing hall and all other details were listed in the pantomime programme including an artist's impression of the proposed new hall [see sketch below]PROG

Oct Neston County Council bought 22 acres of land in Liverpool Road **Neston** which had been used by the Ministry of Health, the Royal Navy and evacuees from flying bombs in London 1944 NW

Left: *The thatched roof of the **Irby** Village Post Office, behind the lamp post, is in a dangerous state. It was replaced with a corrugated iron one and became the doctor's surgery with the Post Office moving to the far right shop [see 1950]*

Above: *The Heatherlands Cafe is seen in Thurstaston Road **Thurstaston** with School Lane to the right. During the Second World War this building was used by the Ministry of Food as a food storage depot. The Heatherlands Restaurant, with its distinctive 1930s design, is still thriving today. Just to the left of the photo was the Heatherland Garage*

Above: *This was an artist's view of the proposed new extended Irby Village Hall Thingwall Road **Irby**. The original hall was opened in 1938 on a freehold site given by Miss L Lee Townsend [later Mrs Colley] at a cost of over £2,000. The extended hall would have been double the floor space of the original and would have seated over 400 people. It was proposed to included a complete, effective stage with dressing rooms, a foyer entrance, cloakrooms and improved kitchen area. The total cost would have been £5,000 - sadly the extension never took place. The hall's claim to fame came 16 years later when the Beatles appeared here for the Newton Dancing School 7 September 1962* PROG

1948

- Miss Lois Bulley presented *Mickell Brow* and gardens at **Ness** to the University of **Liverpool** on condition that the gardens should be kept as a practical and fitting tribute to her father[N]
- *Dale Farm* **Barnston** opened as a residential camp by the Liverpool Boys Association[BPV]
- **Burton** Manor sold by Alfred Joynson to **Liverpool** City Council who acted on behalf of a consortium of local authorities in the region - then used as a residential college for adult education[BM]
- **Irby** Cricket Club was formed - their home ground was in Seaview Lane Irby. They bought land off Dodd's Farm in Mill Hill Road in 1968 and it has been their home ever since
- **Liverpool** Savings Bank opened a branch in Telegraph Road **Heswall**[SOUV]

Jan 1   Railways nationalised - now all part of British Railways[APWR]

Above: *The West Wirral Division of the Cheshire County Constabulary Police Headquarters are seen in Hinderton Road **Neston***

Above: *This was one of many holiday cabins built on land belonging to Quarry Farm on **Irby** Mill Hill*

Below: ***Irby** Village is seen from Irby Manor grounds. Manor Farm, which was an Elizabethan building, is seen to the left of the tree. Unfortunately it became derelict and although it was initially saved from being demolished - it was taken down in 1967. Irby Library and public toilets being built on land behind the farmhouse [see 1960]. 'Broster's corner' is seen on the right in Irby Road.and behind the right of the cars parked in Thingwall Road is a BP petrol sign - this was originally the smithy and later became an estate agent's office*

Above: *The Margaret Bevan Home for girls is pictured at the bottom of Riverbank Road **Lower Heswall**. Formerly St Fillans' Preparatory School for Boys [see 1926]. The girls wore matching coats and berets*

1949

– **Irby** Methodist Church purchased an organ for £1,380[SOUV]
– The **Irby** Telephone Exchange opened in a purpose-built building at No.37 Whalley Lane with over 300 subscribers
– First post-war houses built at Rose Gardens off Badger Bait **Little Neston**, plus Mellock Lane and Raeburn Avenue **Neston**[NW]
– Morgan Crucible established on a 45 acre site north of Liverpool Road **Neston** where they eventually employed 500 workers producing insulating firebricks, refractory cements and other similar industrial products[NW]
Feb 20 The first part of the Second World War Memorial in the form of a new altar rail was dedicated at Christ's Church **Barnston**[SOUV]

Above: *Gordale was founded on the Chester High Road at* **Burton** *in 1948 by Albert and Lilian Whittaker with their daughter Joyce and her husband Harold Nicholson, the five acre smallholding cost £9,500 [a large amount of money then]. They sold their produce from this shed, erected in 1949, fronting onto Chester High Road. It had a bell and an honesty box as the family were busy in the gardens most of the time [see 1953]*

Above: *Looking from the* Royal Oak Inn **Little Neston** *towards the Green on the left. Behind the car is a 'modern' telephone box and the houses to the right were called* Hope Cottages

Above: *The sea wall on The Parade at* **Parkgate** *is almost hidden from view by the high tide with the seats on the Donkey stand under water - a car in the distance is passing Mostyn House School [the half-timbered building]*

1950

– The school attached to Christ Church **Barnston** was moved to temporary accommodation in Storeton Lane - the school building was renovated and opened in 1952 as the church hall[SOUV]

– **Parkgate** Swimming Baths closed [see 1932][YW1]

Aug 7 The annual **Heswall** Horse and Horticultural Show held on the Glegg Estate land opposite the *Glegg Arms*, Chester High Road **Gayton** [see advert and map etc on this page and next page][PROG]

Above: *Nicholls' Ice Cream Parlour is seen on the right on The Parade at* **Parkgate**

Above: *The building on the right was the* Kings Cinema *Telegraph Road* **Heswall** *seen in 1950 with the poster advertising Alan Ladd in* After Midnight. *The* Kings Hall *was built in 1912, it became the station for John Pye's bus service [see 1921] and having provided limited cinema entertainments for 16 years, in 1928 John Pye decided to upgrade it to meet demand from a growing population. From the mid 1930s it changed hands several times - during the war the cinema was used as a centre for issuing ration books - and by the time this photograph was taken it was part of the SM Super Cinema circuit. It was purchased by the Essoldo group in 1954 but the cinema closed in 1958 and the building bought by Lennons Supermarkets in 1960. The white circles on the traffic light pole and telegraph pole on the left were a legacy from the black-out precautions during the war, another legacy was the lack of cars due to rationing of petrol and new cars*

Below: *This was an advert in the August Bank Holiday Show programme [see opposite]*

Above: *Part of the* Barn End Cottage *roof in* **Burton** *has been re-thatched. Built on a sandstone outcrop it was once a beerhouse known as the* Fisherman's Arms *[in 1561 Burton had five licensed houses but by 1861 there were none] and more recently* Noah's Ark[B]

106

Above: *The car on the left has just left Mill Hill Road and is seen being driven into Thingwall Road **Irby**. K Matthews' Elm Tree Stores is to the left and beyond the next two-storied cottages is the former single-storied Post Office whose thatched roof was replaced with a tin one [due to shortage of building materials after the Second World War] and became Dr Barnes' Surgery. Constantine grocers shop is the nearest of the row of shops then Jones' chemist shop, Birkenhead Co-op branch and the Post Office at the far end. The* Prince of Wales Inn *had been demolished with the site eventually becoming the car park. The first building on the right, with a car parked outside, was the library until the present one was opened in 1967 [see 1960]*

Above: *This was the programme cover for the 1950 '**Heswall** and District Annual Horse and Horticultural Show' held at **Gayton** [see below]*

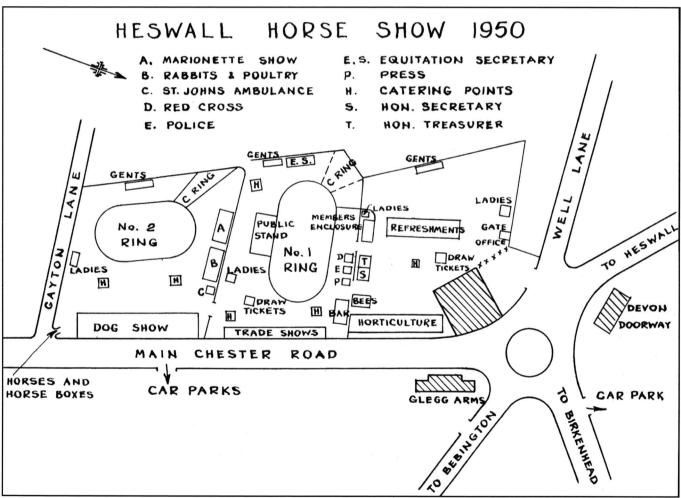

Above: *This map shows the location of the '**Heswall** and District Horse and Agricultural Show' on the Chester High Road **Gayton** which was on Glegg Estate land opposite the* Glegg Arms. *The entertainment at the August Bank Holiday event included: show jumping and other horse events [there were two show rings]; a dog show; rabbit show; display by the British Alsation Training Club; marionette show; honey show; an horticultural show with 116 classes including flowers, fruit and vegetables; music and entertainment by the Pipers and Dancers of the Liverpool Scottish [TA] and trade shows. Unfortunately the poultry show had to be cancelled due to the outbreak of fowl pest in the area*

1951

- Coombe Road Primary School **Irby** opened - taking many pupils from **Dawpool** School which had become overcrowded
- The Palfreyman family's 105 years of keeping the *Harp Inn* **Ness**, ended[NEWS]

Above: *This Crosville Leyland Titan TD5 bus, No. M67 - registration No. CFM 369, is pictured in the **Heswall** bus station on 17 February 1951. This operated on the **Birkenhead** to Heswall route via **Pensby***

Above: *The whole of the village seems to have turned out in High Street **Neston** for the Neston Ladies' Club procession which is passing Appleton's chandlery and hardware shop on the left. This annual event, which dates back to 1814, is still held on every first Thursday in June [see 1914]*

Above: *The S4 - Beadle-bodied 28 seat Bedford OB bus - 6-cylinder petrol engine was new in 1947 and bought as a stop gap when new buses were hard to come by. It operated on the Banks Road local service and is seen here outside Broadway Stores in Broad Lane at the junction of Banks Road **Heswall**. The single-decker bus not only provided locals with a service to and from Heswall bus station but also visitors who wanted to enjoy the sands at Heswall and would gain access to the shore at the bottom of Banks Road by the Dee Sailing Club [later* Sheldrakes]

Above: *This post-war photograph of The Parade **Parkgate** still showed the white line painted on the land side of the sea wall, on the pavement and the black and white painted post on the corner of* Dee Cottages - *all were used to guide pedestrians and drivers during the black-out*

Left: *Two children are playing in the doorway of a single-storied thatched cottage on the right and a lady is seen beyond in front of a two-storied thatched cottage in **Ness** village. Both these cottages were demolished and replaced with houses built in Smithy Close. The row of three cottages to the right of the lorry are still there today. The far building on the other side of the road was* The Old Bakery *and to the right, behind the tall tree was the* Wheatsheaf Inn *[see 1960]*

Above: *The* Deeside cafe *is the distinctive black and white building on the left which later became a Chinese restaurant. The car on the left is by Mostyn square and Mostyn House School is the tall building in the background. The name Mostyn commemorates the Mostyn family who owned the whole village of* **Parkgate** *from 1672 until 1849 when all their family estates in Cheshire were sold at auction*

Above: *This 1950s photograph shows the interior of the Birkenhead Brewery* Glegg Arms **Gayton.** *This was the public bar - mainly the domain of men - with ladies more at home in the lounge bar [see 1959]*

Left: *This was the single-tracked* **Hooton** *to* **West Kirby** *railway line looking towards* **Parkgate,** *where it passed* **Heswall** *Golf Club. The main course and clubhouse were on the left and to the right of the bend in the railway line were the six holes the Dee side of the line. The railway line closed to passengers in 1956 and to goods in 1962. Cheshire County Council purchased most of the trackbed in 1969 and it now forms part of the Wirral Way with the Visitor Centre opening at* **Thurstaston** *in 1973*

Right: *The main landmark in this aerial view of* **Burton** *Village is the Parish Church of St Nicholas [top centre] with its cemetery in front and to the left. This is one village that has changed little over the centuries with the population in 1801 being 288 [***Birkenhead** *at that time was 110] and by 1921 it had decreased by six to 282 [Birkenhead by then had increased to 145,577].*

1952

Nov   The second part of the Second World War
Memorial dedicated at Christ's Church **Barnston**
in the form of a new font ^{SOUV}[see February 1949]

Above: *The sign for Mostyn House School Parkgate is seen above the single-storey building and on the roof is the air-raid siren which was used during the Second World War to warn residents of Parkgate that there was an imminent air raid. The siren at* **Neston** *was initially on the roof of the Town Hall but later moved to the Police Station and the one at* **Burton** *was on the Burton Manor roof. The sirens were operated by the local police with the noise travelling many miles. Nicholls' Ice Cream shop is seen above the near cars*

Above: *Looking down High Street* **Neston**, *the Town Hall is out of picture to the left of the near car. The first shop seen on the left was George Mason's grocer's shop with its van parked in front. The former* Neston Hotel *was on the right - originally known as* The Vaults *and then changed to* The Letters - *it was demolished in 1931*

Left: *Neston Mill looks as though it needed a coat of paint. Standing in Leighton Road* **Neston** *it was last worked in the 1880s. It was restored in 1975 and became* The Old Mill Gallery *operating a glass engraving business from here until 1990*

The Devon Doorway

Licensed Restaurant

Heswall   **Cheshire**

Telephone : HES 717

MORNING COFFEES   LUNCHES

AFTERNOON and HIGH TEAS

All Types of Party Catering

WEDDINGS   BIRTHDAY PARTIES
DINNER OR   BUFFET   DANCES
OFFICE PARTIES   HOT-POT SUPPERS etc

Under Personal Supervison of the Proprietor

Above: *Advert for the* Devon Doorway Restaurant **Gayton** *[see left]*

Above: *This was* **Neston** *Cross with Westminster Bank to the left of the car then to the right was Ernest Benson, Fruiterer.*

Left: The Devon Doorway *Restaurant at* **Gayton** *[see above] with a new roundabout in front. Barnston Road is to the right*

1953

- **Heswall** Council Mixed Council School became known as Heswall County Primary School[TSP]
- **Heswall** Society established[SOUV]

Jun 2 **Coronation of Queen Elizabeth II**

Dec 7 A sun lounge and garden of remembrance was opened at the rear of **Neston** Library in memory of those local men who died in the 1939-45 war[NW]

Above: *The procession for the Ladies Day Walk is proceeding down High Street **Neston** and passing the junction of Brook Street on the right with Irwins grocery shop on the corner [later became Tesco]. Now known as The Neston Female Society, it was founded in 1814 and still celebrates on the first Thursday in June[YW6]*

Above: *Parkgate was very busy with people out for a stroll along the promenade. The two shops on the left were the Hilo Espresso coffee bar and The Green Leaf Cafe. The modern 1930s building next door was opened c1937 with three units - Grace Brook, [here - The Wool Shop]; Nicholls' Milk Bar and Ice Cream Parlour with access to the balcony via stairs at the back of the cafe - the heads of customers can be seen on the balcony above the shop [here - still Nicholls Cafe - see text 1937]; third shop Bensons.The Crosville bus is passing in front of the* Union Hotel *later to become the* Ship Inn *and Mostyn House School is the tall building beyond*

Above: *The two girls are on the marshes with **Parkgate** in the background. Nicholls' Milk Bar and Ice Cream Parlour is seen on the left and the Custom House on the far right*

Above: *The children of Mrs Ellis' Everleigh School in Coombe Road **Irby** have dressed up and are celebrating the Coronation of Queen Elizabeth II on 2 June*

Above: *This was part of Gordale Nurseries on the Chester High Road, **Burton,** bought in 1948 by the Whittaker and Nicholson families [see page 105]. This two-bedroomed dorma bungalow, probably built in the 1930s, was included in the purchase of the five acre site - it has been altered somewhat and it is still lived in today. The sign for 'Teas and Hovis' fronting onto Chester High Road advertised the cafe which was the glass structure seen surrounding the house. This seated about 60 people and was popular with walkers, cyclists [many from **Liverpool**] and visitors to **Parkgate**. They were well known for their chicken salads, especially as food rationing was still in place and this was a way that families could enjoy food over and above their ration allowances. There was a garage there when the site was purchased, which was not part of Gordale, but was owned and run by Frank Howard. He sold it to a third party but it was eventually bought by Gordale in 1984, by which time neighbouring land had also been purchased - Gordale was then 23 acres [see 1959]*

Above: *The station sign for Neston North on the Mid Wirral line is seen on the left. From when it opened in 1896 until 1952 it was known simply as **Neston** Railway Station. In 1952, to avoid confusion with the other station in Neston half a mile away, it was re-named Neston North - it took long enough to realise there was a problem! Neston South on the **Hooton** to **West Kirby** line closed to passengers in 1956 and to freight in 1962. Neston North - now just Neston still operates today on the Wrexham line*

Above: *This open-air Church service was held at The Cross **Neston** on Rogation Sunday [the Sunday before Ascension Day]. Irwins Modern grocers shop is seen behind the congregation on the corner of Brook Street and the shop to the right was the Neston Wine and Spirit Store*

Above: *Looking up Thurstaston Road **Irby** towards the village. Laburum Cottage was to the left*

1954

- New Post Office built in Pensby Road **Heswall**[YW1]
- **Heswall** Operatic Society performed *Veronique*
- The Raby Road Estate **Neston** was completed[NW]
- *Elder Cottage* opposite the *Black Horse Hotel* **Lower Heswall** demolished and the road widened [see 1958][YW6]

Jan 11   A memorial screen bearing the names of those who died in the Second World War was unveiled in **Neston** Parish Church - including WL Bee, who was lost at sea in 1942, whose father was the former Police Sergeant at **Neston** [see 1920][NW]

Feb 1   **Thurstaston** and **Caldy** stations closed on the **Hooton** to **West Kirby** railway line

Jul 3   Summer fair held on the Puddydale **Heswall** to raise money for the Clever Chapel Fund. Events included:- March Past and Tattoo; Baby Show; Physical Training Display; Crowning the Queen of the Fair and Puppet Theatre [PROG]

Above: *Cinema House was one of two shops in the King's Cinema building Telegraph Road **Heswall**. It advertised 'high quality chocolates and sweets, cigarettes and library'. They also sold Reece's ice cream, greetings cards and postcards. The shop was run by DW White from 1934 to 1958 [see 1950]*

Above: *The Post office, which is a modern extension to an old stone cottage, is seen in The Village **Burton**. In 1896 there was no Post Office in Burton - only a wall letter box which was cleared at 6pm except 11.20am on Sundays. By 1906 there was a Post Office with Mrs Martha Cotterell as Sub-Postmistress. The Post Office and shop closed some years ago and is now a private house [see 1935]*

Above: *This was **Neston** South Station on the **Hooton** to **West Kirby** line which opened in 1866 - the station opened the same year and was then called simply Neston. In 1952, to avoid confusion with the other station in Neston half a mile away, it was re-named Neston South. The building jutting out with the bay window was the station master's house. This station closed to passengers in 1956 and to freight in 1962 with the old track bed here becoming part of the Wirral Country Park*

Left: *Boys are playing football on the Puddydale **Heswall**. The buildings in the background were Heswall Primary School, founded in 1909 as the Council School. The school transferred to Whitfield Lane in 1976 and was known as Whitfield Primary School - in 1992 it became Heswall Primary School*

Right: *The bunting and flags are out at Two Mills Motor Co garage to celebrate the Coronation of Queen Elizabeth II. Seen at the Welsh Crossroads - the chimney to the right belonged to the Tudor Rose [see 1939]. The AA and RAC men saluted members at these crossroads*

Above: *Looking up the High Street **Neston** the* White Horse Inn *is behind the* Bushell Fountain *on the left with the* Brown Horse Inn *on the right. The car on the right is parked by the two Esso petrol pumps belonging to the garage*

Left: *The cottage on the right at **Parkgate** dated back to the 1720s. It was the Custom House from 1799 to 1828 and so named the Watch House. The upturned boat on the left on the Middle Slip was a relic from when fish were landed here [see 1938]. As the Dee silted up fishermen caught their fish towards **Hilbre Island***

Above: *This aerial view of the Royal Liverpool Children's Hospital **Heswall** was taken after the Second World War as the tall building top left facing onto Telegraph Road originally had two houses next door but they were destroyed by bombs on the night of 30 May 1941 - they are empty spaces here, but the ambulance station was later built on the site. The house top left of the Puddydale was* Southwood *and the two cottages top right were demolished with shops and car park built on the site*

1955

– The Children's Church [opposite the *Black Horse*] **Lower Heswall**, which had been used as a library, was restored in memory of R Mellor [see 1958]NEWS

– The Wirral Players celebrated their 10th anniversary with the pantomime "The Old Lady Who Lived in a Shoe" at **Irby** Village HallPROG

Mar 23 For four days **Neston** Operatic Society performed *Tom Jones* which was to be their last performance - in their Golden Jubilee yearPROG

Nov 24 Ian Terrance Botham [the cricketer] - now Sir Ian - was born in Oldfield Way **Heswall**

Dec 5 **Burton** Point station closed on the **Bidston** to **Wrexham** railway line

Above: Balcony House, *which is seen on the left on The Parade **Parkgate** was late 18th century and originally two houses, it is now flats - the balcony dates from between 1860 and 1880*TP

Left: *Looking along Barnston Road **Barnston**, the Post Office is seen to the right of the light-coloured telephone box. The finger post in the centre is pointing towards Storeton Lane where the Barnston Camp was situated [see below]*

Above: Dale House Farm *Storeton Lane* **Barnston** *had been a popular venue for picnics and Sunday school outings [see 1925]. It was opened by the Liverpool Boys' Association in 1948 as a residential camp which had accommodation in four huts sleeping 88 and eight twin rooms for the leaders*

Above: *Although grass had taken over on the once sandy beach at **Parkgate**, the tide often lapped the sea wall*

Above: *The west front of the* Leighton Hotel *[see advert top left] is seen in Boathouse Lane* **Parkgate**. *Once a girls' school [see 1918] and more recently the* Parkgate Hotel - *it then became a private residence*

Above left: *This was an advert for the* Leighton Hotel *Boathouse Lane* **Parkgate** *[seen above] when MA Oakes was the proprietor. It was described as "Comfortable residential hotel in secluded grounds. Spacious lounges, sunny conservatory, TV lounge. All bedrooms fitted with electric fires and H & C water"*

Above: *Looking down High Street* **Neston** *the Crosville bus is waiting outside the* White Horse Inn *on the right; Rostances shop is behind The Cross; The* Brown Horse Inn *is on the left and Irwins Grocers shop beyond*

Below: *This picturesque photograph of a beached yacht was taken on the shore at* **Heswall** *when there was plenty of sand and no grass*

Above: *The centre of* **Heswall** *is seen where Telegraph Road was straight ahead, on the left the District Bank was on the corner of Pensby Road, then next door Lloyd's Chemist and the* Kings Cinema *beyond [see 1950] - Lloyds' Bank on the right was on the corner of The Mount*

Above: *The* Broad Beams Cafe,- *the black and white half-timbered building on The Parade* **Parkgate**, *was advertised on this postcard. This row of 18th century houses had bay windows added in the 19th century and black and white decoration in the 20th century*

1956

– **Neston** County Council had provided 500 houses by this date[NW]

– *Holywell Hotel* The Parade **Parkgate** became the first residential home for elderly diabetics in the north of England[YW6]

Feb 16 The Akbar Nautical Training School **Heswall** closed [see 1926 and 1957][YW]

Sep 15 Stations on the **Hooton** to **West Kirby** railway line closed[YW6]

Sep 17 **Hooton** to **West Kirby** railway line closed to passengers but stayed open to goods traffic until 1962[APWR]

Dec Plans were completed for constructing Fishers Lane between Irby Road and Pensby Road **Pensby**[NEWS]

Above: *The railway official is waiting, with a staff in his hand, for the train approaching **Parkgate** Station on the **Hooton** to **West Kirby** line [see below]*
Below: *The train driver is receiving one staff and handing over another at **Parkgate** Station. These staffs were used on the single-line track to prevent two trains travelling in opposite direction on the same stretch of track. However, this did not prevent the accident at **Thurstaston** [see 1957]*

Above: *This was one of the competitors in the Show Jumping competition at the **Heswall** Show which took place on August Bank Holiday Monday - the site being on the Chester High Road opposite the Glegg Arms **Gayton** [see 1950]*

Below: *The shops on the right in Castle Buildings Telegraph Road **Heswall** are from the right: Atherton's - cafe; National Coal Board; Riley's - fruit and vegetables; Chas. E Price - electrical goods, LE Jones - further down was Goulds - printers and stationers. There were cottages behind the trees on the left which have been replaced by a row of shops*

Right: *The Church of the Good Shepherd is on the right in Telegraph Road **Heswall** and a Crosville bus is entering the bus depot in the distance*

Left: *Taken from the tower of St Peter's Church **Lower Heswall**, the houses in the foreground were in Rectory Lane - with the two on the right in the process of being built. Beyond these houses and fronting the River Dee was Park West with the Welsh hills beyond.*

Right: *Looking up School Lane **Thurstaston,** which was a cul-de-sac off Thurstaston Road, by the Heatherlands Cafe. The road was named after Dawpool School whose chimneys and roof can be seen behind the white painted house on the left. The school, which was largely funded by Margaret Ismay, was opened here in 1906. Hillside Farm, which was further up the lane on the right, was popular with ramblers and picnicers [see 1934]*

Above: *This was an aerial view of the Akbar Approved Nautical Training School in Green Lane off Oldfield Drive **Heswall**. This shows their football pitch and bottom left was a model of a ship. In 1944 Lieutenant-Commander Martin Johnson, who had been awarded the George Medal for defusing four torpedoes from a captured U-boat, was appointed Deputy Captain and then Captain in 1950. Under his guidance a disciplined but enlightened programme which involved practical seamanship, cooking and stewarding, as well as schoolroom lessons, meant that the majority of the boys were enabled to lead normal lives after leaving. In the first three years after leaving - 83% of his boys remained out of trouble. This was one of six approved schools that were closed down in 1956 [see 1926]*

1957

–   A row blew up in **Neston** over the Council's refusal of the Municipal Buildings' Committee to allow a jazz concert in Neston Institute on a Sunday[NEWS]

Jan   The demolition of part of the former Akbar Nautical Training School was approved with a planning application for residential development on the land at the bottom of Oldfield Drive **Heswall** [see 1956][NEWS]

Feb 25   The only recorded accident on the **Hooton** to **West Kirby** line occurred when two freight trains collided head-on at **Thurstaston** Station with only minor injuries suffered [see photo next page][YW6]

Mar 30   Foundation stone laid for St Michael and All Angels Church **Pensby**[SOUV]

Jul 11   The **Hooton** to **West Kirby** branch line received its most important train ever when the full Royal Train transported the Queen and Duke of Edinburgh. The Duke left the train at **Ledsham** and the Queen continued on to **Wallasey**[THWKBL]

Above: *New Street Ness is seen from a slag heap left over from when the colliery which ceased operating in 1927. There were 20 purpose built cottages, dating from the late 1870s seen on the far side of New Street which had two large rooms downstairs and two bedrooms upstairs - there was a long communal shed at the back which housed the toilets [see 1878]. The row of 18 cottages opposite [to the right] were known as 'parlour' houses as they were bigger than those opposite and had a parlour, still having two bedrooms. This was a very close community of miners and their families in 38 cottages who did not like 'foreigners' and they even had their own shop - this was next to the alleyway [the dark gap between the far cottages]. The open area, opposite the cottages on the left, was known as 'drying land' which is where washing would be hung out and it was also used as allotments - especially during the two wars*

Above: *Looking along Village Road **Lower Heswall**, the shops from the left were: The Shop - wool, sweets, tobacco; Reegans - shoe maker; Herbert Gill, Post Office - stationery, cigarettes, fancy goods, toys etc; Fred Coles - ironmonger; W Hall - garage, service station and taxis. Opposite: the van on the right is on the corner of The Lydiate outside A Burke - newsagent tobacconist and high class confectioner*

Below: *The man is inspecting the remnants of an old mine shaft. The shaft and slag heap on the left, were relics of mining at **Little Neston** which ceased in 1927. The end building seen on the extreme right in New Street is also seen above. The building to the right of the man was known as the Salt Box and at one time lived in by Tom and Maud Tudor. Houses were built from the 1970s on the site of this area surrounding Neston Colliery and in the 1980s on the site of the earlier **Ness** Collieries, behind the Harp Inn*

Left: *This was a view looking down Glenwood Drive **Irby** with the two houses either side being in Thingwall Road. At this time it was a quiet, leafy road with only Woodside Road, Linwood Drive and fields off Glenwood Drive. However, following a housing development in the 1960s, Glenwood Drive was extended, linking up with Coombe Road [see 1937]*

1957 continued

Above: *This was the result of the only recorded collision on the Wirral line from **Hooton** to **West Kirby**. The accident took place at **Thurstaston** Station on 25 February 1957 when two freight trains collided head-on. Both trains and four wagons were derailed - three of those on board the trains suffered minor injuries[YW6]*

Above: *The building on the right is at the junction of Mostyn Square [to the right] and The Parade **Parkgate**. Leeman's Garage had been sited at the end of these buildings for many years but in 1957 sold out to Regent Oil whose sign can be seen at the front. Beyond the garage was once the Parkgate Convalescent Home which dated back to 1882. It was used during both wars as a military hospital and demolished in the 1950s*

Above: *The Harp Inn at **Little Neston** was the white building on the left and a popular rendezvous for the yachts which had sailed here from **Hoylake** Sailing Club - Dee Sailing Club also used this venue. It was a Birkenhead Brewery pub and described in one of their publications c.1960 as "steeped in antiquity - known as the wildfowlers' public house, the Old Harp Inn stands on marshland near the site of the old Wirral Colliery - the ceilings are low and supported by oak beams, which are believed to be the original used in its 17th century construction - the present licensee Mr TR Johnson took over the inn in 1951 from Mr Palfreyman whose family had held the licence for 105 years" [see 1909]*

Above: *This was the interior of the Spinning Wheel Cafe which was situated at 78 Telegraph Road **Heswall**. They advertised: 'For excellent lunches teas grills etc - home-made cakes - private room for function - telephone Heswall 1687'*

Above: *Len Parry's Motor Cycle shop was situated in Pensby Road **Heswall** for many years*

1958

–   *Kings Cinema*, ballroom and two adjoining shops Telegraph Road **Heswall** failed to sell at auction - reserve was £7,500. It was later bought by Lennon's Supermarkets of St Helens and in 1960 plans were approved to convert the former cinema into a supermarket[TSSW]

–   Neston Market, which dated back 1728 when granted a Charter by George II, was reopened by the council as an indoor Market at Neston Institute, after a lapse [now Neston Civic Hall] - it continued to be run here until August 1965 when it was relocated under the Town Hall.

Jan 6   **Neston** County Secondary Modern School opened in Raby Park Road[NW]

Feb 8   St Michael and All Angels Church Pensby Road **Pensby** dedicated[SOUV]

Above: *The Dee Sailing Club boats are seen on the sands near their clubhouse on **Heswall** shore. The club was founded as the Heswall Sailing Club in 1909 and a clubhouse was built on land at the bottom of Banks Road at a cost of £65. It changed its name to the Dee Sailing Club in 1912 and a new clubhouse was built in the 1920s on the other side of Banks Road. Following a successful Coronation Regatta in 1937, a new wooden clubhouse was officially opened in 1938. In 1961 an extension to the clubhouse and starter's box were completed*

Left: *The boats of Dee Sailing club are seen from the other direction to the photograph above. However, due to silting, the Dee Sailing Club moved its racing to **Thurstaston** and eventually moved their moorings as well - with a new clubhouse opened there in 1982[TDSC]*

Above: *The Black Horse Hotel is seen on the right at the junction of Village Road **Lower Heswall** and School Lane. Built in 1872 it was originally called The Black Horse Hotel but when Mr Leeman became the licensee in 1898 it was known as the Heswall Hotel. It reverted to its former name in 1940. The building on the left was once the library, being restored in memory of Geoffrey Mellor, then became a children's church. Beyond the church was Elder Cottage dating back to 1686, which housed the school until it moved to School Hill in 1872. It was demolished in 1954 and the road was later widened[YW6]*

Above: *This photograph shows how quickly the River Dee silted up at **Parkgate** with the last small inlet on the right. However, the high tides did cover the grass and lap against the sea wall [see 1955].*

Above: *This was a view of the newly built Raby Road Housing Estate at* **Neston***. By the end of 1958, the Urban District Council of Neston had erected 739 houses and flats - all but 82 were post-war construction with further development planned. At the same time there were 394 private houses erected post-war in the Neston area*

Above: Leighton Court *Neston [see 1916] is advertised here as a 'Residential Country Club'. However, it was a very popular venue in the 1960s and 70s as a night club and was at one time Wirral's only licenced gambling casino*

Above: *The* Royal Oak Inn *is seen looking across The Green at* **Little Neston***. This Birkenhead Brewery pub was rebuilt in 1901 replacing the original one which had been destroyed by fire. The pub dated back to at least 1822 when the licensee was Samuel Hancock [see 1893 and 1903]*

Above: *This air-view of* **Burton** *Village shows St Nicholas' Church and graveyard to the left - above the trees. The main road in the village can be seen in front of the church*

1959

– Anne Thelwell from **Heswall** won the Miss United Kingdom title
– **Heswall** AFC joined the West Cheshire League
– The Parish of **Barnston** was extended to include **Thingwall** which had previously been in the Parish of **Woodchurch**[SOUV]
– **Little Neston** School became an infants school called Ness Holt School[N]

May 11 **Parkgate** and **Neston** Presbyterian Church struck by lightening and caused a fire - luckily it was discovered and was put out without too much damage[SOUV]

Above: *The boy is about to dive into the open-air swimming pool at the Heswall Boys' Camp Broad Lane Heswall [at the bottom of Delavor Road]. This four acre site was opened in 1934 for the Merseyside Youth Association. A new complex was later built in memory of Tommy Handley [a former Liverpool Comedian], which housed an indoor swimming pool, squash court and gymnasium [see 1937]*

Above: *The* Wheatsheaf Inn *at* **Ness** *was rebuilt in the 1920s and a Birkenhead Brewery publication c.1960 describes it thus: "A fine cocktail bar has recently been installed, with views over a pleasing garden and the hillside sweeping down to the River Dee, with the enchanting back-drop of the Welsh hills. Like most Birkenhead Brewery houses it has adequate car parking facilities for those motorists who know the delightful scenery through which one drives when coming here from all parts of Wirral. Mrs C Marsh came to the* Wheatsheaf Inn *towards the end of 1959 and her house provides a regular rendezvous for the Wheatsheaf and Ness Villager's Darts Club" [see 1922]*

Above: *The first licensee of the* Glegg Arms *at* **Gayton** *was Edward Crabbe who was also a wheelwright. The* **Birkenhead** *Brewery booklet of the 1950s describes the pub thus: "Today the inn typifies the solace to be derived from visiting a typical village pub. The clean, well kept front of the building has a pleasant glass-roofed verandah, under which there are bench seats looking onto the road [sounds idyllic!]. The inn has two congenial bars, the lounge and public [see 1951] in which snacks and sandwiches may also be obtained. During the summer months customers can enjoy their drinks in an adjoining beer garden or relax with a game of bowls on the green attached to the inn [see 1915]"[WDW]*

Above: *Gordale Nurseries shop is seen on the Chester High Road* **Burton**. *This photograph, taken on the first day of the new greenhouse opening with the 'shoppers' being the owners Lilian Whittaker in the shop and Joyce Nicholson with her son Peter outside [see 1953]*

Above: *The Wirral Urban District Council bought* Hill House *off Telegraph Road* **Heswall** *[seen here] - which became the Council offices - together with some five acres of land which were laid out with tennis courts, an 18 hole putting green and a bowling green. Originally the Council were interested in buying Heswall Castle [see 1915] but having fallen into disrepair and especially due to the flat roof - it would have cost too much to repair. Hill House is currently the* Jug and Bottle *hotel and restaurant*

1960

– **National Service ended**
– The **Birkenhead** Brewery Company applied for planning permission to demolish the *Custom House* - a Georgian building at the south end of the promenade at **Parkgate** and develop the site with gardens for a new public house which was to replace the *Chester Hotel* [see photos]*NEWS*
– Plans to demolish the Custom House at **Parkgate** were initially passed by the Neston Planning Committee but the main Council decided to refer the matter back to the committee [see photos and details below]
– Irwins with 212 stores - many branches in Wirral - was taken over by Tesco

– Plans for an extension to the Dee Sailing Club at **Heswall** were approved - completed in 1961 [due to further silting of the Dee, a new clubhouse was opened at **Thurstaston** in 1982]*SOUV*
– *Thingwall Hall* on the corner of Pensby Road and Barnston Road demolished [see 1920]
– *Manor Farm* Thingwall Road **Irby** condemned - later demolished [see photo below]*YW6*
– St Peter's Church of England Primary School opened Thurstaston Road **Heswall**
Apr 23 *Neston New Cinema* closed - reopened as the *Royal Cinema* 13 November 1961*YW6*
May Plans to convert the *Kings Cinema* Telegraph Road **Heswall** into a self-service supermarket and coffee bar were approved*NEWS*

Above: *Thingwall Road* **Irby** *is seen to the right with a service road to the left which was originally a short section of dual carriageway with mini roundabout - mainly used by learner drivers over the years. The houses in the distance were built c.1937 by Costains at Parkway [see 1937] who bought the land off Lord Leverhulme's Arrowe Estate which he had acquired in 1919 - this was the initial development of the land here. The next phase was to build over 800 houses on land to the left - from here to Arrowebrook Lane with shops planned to face the road here. The Second World War intervened and the development was put on hold, with the service road the only sign of the estate that was never built*

Above: Manor Farm *seen on the left in Thingwall Road* **Irby**, *which was owned by the Council, was condemned in 1960 as the building was in a dangerous condition. However, the Wirral Society and other local bodies had the order withdrawn in 1962. Despite this and due to lack of repairs to the damaged building, this delightful Elizabethan farmhouse was demolished in 1967. The library and public conveniences were built on the site [see 1950].The row of shops to the right of the tall tree included a branch of Irwins grocery stores [they were taken over by Tesco in 1960]*

Left: *Birkenhead* Brewery, who owned the Chester Arms *at* **Parkgate**, *submitted plans to demolish the* Cosy Cafe, *[building on right] an early 18th century building which had once been the Custom House. They were initially passed by the* **Neston** *Planning Committee. However, the main Council decided to refer the matter back to the Committee and to write to the Georgian Group for more information on the building. The Geogian Group pointed out that the building had been designated by the Ministry of Housing and Local Government as being of architectural and historic interest. It also pointed out that the building played an important role in the street scene and retained some interior features including a fine staircase with Doric column bannisters. All this was to no avail as the building was eventually demolished, the road widened and part of the site became the gardens to the* Old Quay *[see below]NEWS*

Left: *The Birkenhead Brewery pub the* Old Quay *is pictured at* **Parkgate** *when it was newly opened in 1963 [see above]*

INDEX of PHOTOGRAPHS/GRAPHICS

Publications By the Same Author:

Yesterday's Wirral No 1 – Neston, Parkgate & Heswall	by Ian & Marilyn Boumphrey
Yesterday's Wirral No 2 – Birkenhead, Prenton & Oxton	by Ian & Marilyn Boumphrey
Yesterday's Wirral No 3 – West Kirby & Hoylake	by Ian & Marilyn Boumphrey
Yesterday's Wirral No 4 – Wallasey & New Brighton + Leasowe	by Ian & Marilyn Boumphrey
Yesterday's Wirral No 5 – Wallasey, New Brighton & Moreton	by Ian & Marilyn Boumphrey
Yesterday's Wirral No 6 – Neston, Parkgate Heswall + Thurstaston Irby Greasby	by Ian & Marilyn Boumphrey
Yesterday's Wirral No 7 – Birkenhead, Oxton & Prenton + Bidston & Upton	by Ian & Marilyn Boumphrey
Yesterday's Wirral No 8 – Bebington & Mid Wirral Villages	by Ian & Marilyn Boumphrey
Yesterday's Wirral No 9 – Ellesmere Port to Bromborough	by Ian & Marilyn Boumphrey
Yesterday's Wirral Pictorial History 1890 to 1953	by Ian & Marilyn Boumphrey
Yesterday's Wirral Port Sunlight 1888 to 1953	by Ian Boumphrey and Gavin Hunter
Yesterday's Liverpool 1857-1957 [128 pages over 500 photos/graphics]	by Ian Boumphrey
Yesterday's Birkenhead 1860-1960 [128 pages over 550 photos/graphics]	by Ian Boumphrey
Yesterday's Wallasey & New Brighton 1860-1960 [128 pages over 550 photos/graphics]	by Ian Boumphrey
Walking, Cycling & Riding Along the Wirral Way & the Story of the Hooton to West Kirby Railway	by Ian Boumphrey
Birkenhead at War including Bebington 1939-45 – 84 pages - a War Diary with photographs + list of civilians who died	by Ian Boumphrey
Wirral on the Home Front 1939-45 – This 128 page book covers all of Wirral during WWII - including adverts & comic postcards of the time - in full colour	by Ian Boumphrey

By the Same Publisher:

The Funny Side of Wirral Cartoons	by Bill Stott
Another Funny Side of Wirral Cartoons	by Bill Stott
Liverpool Cartoons	by Bill Stott
Liverpool Home Cartoons	by Bill Stott
Liverpool 3 Cartoons	by Bill Stott
Liverpool - Capital of Culture Cartoons	by Bill Stott
The Wirral Country Bus	by TB Maund
The Birkenhead Bus	by TB Maund
The Wallasey Bus	by TB Maund
Shadow to Shadow – History of Bristol Aeroplane Banwell & BAJ	by Stephen Parsons
Birkenhead Electric Trams	by Charles Rycroft
Railway Stations of Wirral	by Mersey Railway History Group
Murder & Mayhem in Birkenhead	by David Malcolm
More Murder & Mayhem in Birkenhead + Wallasey & New Brighton	by David Malcolm & Ian Boumphrey
Walking Through the Blitz in the Birkenhead Area	by NHC Tomlinson
The Story of Mariner's Park Wallasey	by Robert Currams & Mike Condon
Birkenhead Park Cricket Club 1846-1996	by Chris Elston
Medical Matters in Victorian & Edwardian Wallasey	by Dr Richard A Smye
Wallasey at War 1939-45 + List of all civilians who died	by Wallasey Historical Society
Helmets, Handcuffs & Hoses - the Story of the Wallasey Police	by Noel Smith
Helmets, Handcuffs & Hoses - the Story of the Wallasey Fire Brigade	by Noel Smith
Hoylake Racecourse & the Beginnings of the Royal Liverpool Golf Club	by John Pinfold
Beachcombers, Buttercreams and Smugglers' Caves - New Brighton & Liverpool in the 1950s	by Pepe Ruiz

For a Free Catalogue of Wirral Publications which are currently available [several are out of print]
and includes publications by some other local authors - contact the publisher
(some books are sent Post Free in the UK or post at cost abroad)
Ian Boumphrey The Nook 7 Acrefield Road Prenton Wirral CH42 8LD
or Phone: 0151 608 7611 or e-mail: ian@yesterdayswirral.co.uk or visit: www.yesterdayswirral.co.uk

WANTED - The author would be interested to view or Buy any old photographs, postcards,
ephemera, books, souvenir booklets, guides, old newspapers etc.
especially related to Wirral or Liverpool
Also any Gore's, Kelly's or other directories (including telephone directories) pre 1980
especially of Wirral, Liverpool or Cheshire.
Telephone: 0151 608 7611 or e-mail: ian@yesterdayswirral.co.uk